ROBERT J. MOORE

AWARD-WINNING BEST-SELLING AUTHOR

MAGNETIC
ENTREPRENEUR

Don't Judge a Book By Its Cover
Poor Clothes Can Hide a Rich Heart

Legal Disclaimer

Connect with Magnetic Entrepreneur Inc.™
https://www.facebook.com/magneticentrepreneur
www.linkedin.com/in/magneticentrepreneur
E-Mail: magneticpublishing2017@gmail.com

DEDICATION

This book is dedicated to all the courageous entrepreneurs
who take risks and are willing to face
all obstacles and overcome them.
You are the true magnetic ones.

Acknowledgements

First of all, I would like to thank amazing leaders like Les Brown, Raymond Aaron, Bob Proctor, Eric Thomas, Ted McGrath, Mel Robbins, The Ziglar Family, and Kyle Wilson and many more. Not only are they true Magnetic Entrepreneurs, but they freely share their knowledge with others. Without these mentors in my life, I wouldn't be where I am today.

This book series would not be possible without the great contributions of the co-authors. They are real-life examples of people who started out sometimes with nothing and now are not only successful businesspeople but also experts in their own right. Thank you for letting your entrepreneurial spirit shine through and encouraging others by sharing your stories and lessons learned. You are an inspiration to all who will read this book!

To *Steve Siebold*: You are an inspiration to us all. Your ground-breaking work is seen all over the world, and your expertise overall really benefits us all. Thank you for contributing your foreword to this book.

Finally, to you, the reader: No book comes alive until it is read. Thank you for investing in yourself and your future. You will never regret that.

Robert J. Moore

Founder of Magnetic Entrepreneur Inc.™

TABLE OF CONTENTS

Contents

DON'T JUDGE A BOOK BY ITS COVER

FOREWORD

It's been more than 30 years since I was playing tennis on the national junior circuit. After years spent at the University of South Alabama, I went pro, and made my way inside the top 500 world rankings. I was pretty sure my destiny was set, and I'd be spending years taking on names like Connors, McEnroe, Lendl and others. Unfortunately, something was missing. In fact, it was one of the greatest mysteries I had ever encountered, and I became obsessed with trying to figure it out. It kept me up at night and was on my mind 24-hours a day. On some days, I could successfully defeat the world's top-ranked professional tennis players, yet on other days they would completely destroy me.

Where was the consistency? Why were there so many ups and downs? My physical game was as good, if not better, than theirs. I was in the best shape of my life. What was missing?

I began studying the mental aspects of performance, and here was the answer I had been desperately searching for. I didn't have the mental toughness these guys had. I didn't have the discipline it took to be the best day in and day out. I didn't have the mindset needed to be a world-class champion. Unfortunately, by the time I realized this, too much time had gone by. Physically, I couldn't compete against the younger talent. Still in love with the game I grew up playing, I became a coach to junior athletes, and up and coming tennis stars.

For the last 35 years, I've been studying human behaviour, psychological performance and mental toughness of world-class performers in every field, from athletes to executives, Olympians to Navy Seals, and especially entrepreneurs and other super achievers in business. I've also been an entrepreneur for all of these years. Without the lessons in mental toughness I learned on and off the court, I would not be where I am today. I can tell you, without hesitation, there is a major distinction between an entrepreneur and a magnetic entrepreneur.

Allow me to share with you what I have learned about magnetic entrepreneurs. It's not that they are the smartest, most talented or luckiest people in the world. Certainly, all of those things help, but they are not a prerequisite. Instead, being a magnetic entrepreneur has more to do with certain behavioral characteristics, mindset, beliefs and an unwavering passion that never says die.

More specifically, magnetic entrepreneurs are world-class performers in every way imaginable.

- They are committed to personal development and lifelong learning.
- They are professional failures, willing to get knocked down over and over again yet they keep coming back for more, bigger and stronger than ever.
- They understand the difference between logic and emotion. In other words, they operate from logic-based thinking but use emotion to motivate them.
- They use non-linear thinking to solve problems.
- They operate with a sense of urgency, knowing each of us only has a limited amount of time.
- They thrive on world-class self-talk.
- They have a supreme confidence without being cocky.
- They embrace conflict for growth.
- They make do or die commitments.

- They do everything with class.
- They know how to suspend their disbelief.
- They avoid delusion and operate through objective reality.
- They are always thinking big.

In psychological performance training, we use a principle called cocooning. This is where you surround yourself with other world-class performers. They lift you up. They share their lessons of success and failure. They are there to inspire you. They are your community. A book such as this with multiple entrepreneurial stories is a great way you can cocoon yourself and reach a level of greatness and success you never dreamed possible.

I don't know where you are on your journey as an entrepreneur. Whether you are just starting out, someone who has been at it for quite some time and feels stuck, or if you've reached a level of success already, this book can help. It's packed with real-life lessons from other magnetic entrepreneurs waiting to take you under their wing and show you the ropes.

The best news of all is that anyone, and I mean absolutely anyone, can learn to become a magnetic entrepreneur. If you want to succeed in business today, becoming a magnetic entrepreneur is mandatory.

I'm on the sidelines cheering you on. I know you can do it.

All my best,

Steve Siebold

INTRODUCTION

Finding good partners is the key to success in anything:
in business, in marriage and, especially in investing.

– Robert Kiyosaki

Business has dramatically changed in the last twenty years. It is a whole new world out there where there is the opportunity for anyone to grow an amazing business that creates financial freedom. No longer is it only big businesses that make all the money. With the advent of the internet, a whole new environment has been created where anyone with the right skills and training can become successful.

That is where the magnetic entrepreneur comes in. Old-school business techniques no longer work, and just throwing money into television and print ads does not bring the results wanted.

Why?

People are hungry for more. They are tired of being treated like brainless, second-class citizens who mindlessly follow whatever advertising tells them to do. The internet has now given them endless choices on how and where they spend their money. They can do research and make decisions on companies without ever entering their doors. One bad review, from the right person, on the wrong site and their sales can drop dramatically.

Customers and clients are tired of the crap. They want to work with and buy from entrepreneurs and companies that they know, like, and trust. They want to be treated as if they matter. This is why being a magnetic entrepreneur is essential for success in today's world.

You Must Be More

What does it mean to be "magnetic"?

In the Merriam-Webster dictionary (www.merriam-webster.com/ dictionary), it says:

"Possessing an extraordinary power or ability to attract."

Some people naturally have a magnetic personality that does help in business but, if you look at the wording, it also says "ability." That means that there is hope. It is not only naturally gifted people who can succeed; anyone who wants to learn how, can.

But …

You must be willing to become more. That is where most people get stuck. They want to stay the way that they are and reap the rewards of the wealthy. There is a reason why so few people attain it. There is a cost to be a successful entrepreneur: you must become someone you are not.

There are things that you are going to have to let go of, and there are things that you are going to have to master through practice. There is no easy road to prosperity. You must earn it.

What sort of things are you going to have to let go of?

➢ Fear in all forms

➢ Poverty Mindset

➢ Not Enough Mindset

➢ Laziness

➢ Perfectionism

➢ Self-Doubt

These are only a few to get you started. Two hindrances will hold you back from success: what goes on in your head and heart, and the skills and actions you need to get to where you want to go. When you conquer these, success can't help but come to you.

What will you have to master?

Communication Skills

One thing that differentiates successful entrepreneurs from others is their ability to communicate effectively with everyone. They speak carefully and consider their words before they come out of their mouth.

Emotional Control

Things will go wrong in business. The one who overcomes is the one who can control their heart. They don't overreact or take it personally; they step back, take an honest look at the situation, and then come up with a plan to fix things. Which leads to …

Unending Learning

Profound achievers get that way because every roadblock is an opportunity to learn and become more. They recognize that there is a solution to every problem; they just have to figure out what it is.

Sales Skills

You can be an entrepreneur and not know how to sell. However, anything that you do, and you don't sell, is a hobby. You do it because you enjoy it, but you don't necessarily make money from it. In order to be financially successful, especially as a solopreneur, you must be able to sell, or you won't have a business at all; just something you are good at.

Relationship Building Skills

You must recognize that your business will be built upon the relationships that you make with prospects, leads, customers, clients and other entrepreneurs. Each one requires a different skill, and you must master them all. Does it seem overwhelming? Don't let it get to you. Becoming a magnetic entrepreneur is a process that happens over time. You don't learn and implement everything in a week.

That is where all the authors in this book come in. They have "been there" and "done that" and are sharing their knowledge with you. They know the shortcuts and pitfalls that we all experience and are sharing their stories so you can succeed faster than they did.

Each author is an expert who has been at the bottom and worked their way up. Each one had to overcome significant obstacles and become more than they ever could imagine. In the pages of this book, you will learn from them what it means to become a truly magnetic entrepreneur.

Are you ready for an incredible journey? Are you ready to be propelled forward? Then turn the page, and let's get started.

Robert J. Moore

LEARNING NOT TO JUDGE

Robert J Moore

I've had more than my share of being judged. As with most things that hurt, it starts in childhood when character is being formed. In my case, it was being judged and blamed for things like purposely breaking toys when I was innocent of the act.

As a teenager, once I found $5, and mom accused me of stealing it. When I protested that I had REALLY found it, I was threatened with being punished for lying. So, I did what most sensible kids would have done — I said I stole it to avoid punishment.

However, these types of false accusations have a serious negative effect — causing resentment at the injustice that a teenagers feels keenly, damaging my own sense of self-worth. This resentment added to my feelings of anger at the injustice of the situation. I struggled with anger for many years, and finally, when I was in therapy, the therapist said that if anything – my anger would take me down, preventing me from moving forward. Many people who have been unjustly treated have major issues with anger and have to come to a place where they forgive before they can truly heal. To release past hurts and forgive is freeing and has a great positive affect on mental health.

After a number of years with those outside the law, this led later to agreeing to do jail time for others as part of the 'code of honour' for my friends. By this time, my family had basically disowned me anyway and would only think that this was "normal" for me, according to the lifestyle I was living. They would assume that I was getting my 'just reward," never questioning the fact that I may not have been guilty.

However, not only was I judged — I also judged others too. One time up north, I went into a local diner and noticed someone who was dressed in dirty clothes and offered to pay for his meal. He laughed at this and said, "Maybe I should be buying your meal." It turned out that he was the owner of a construction company that was building a big subdivision nearby. He said he enjoyed working right along with his workmen as it made for good morale in his company. That was a very humbling experience, and he did end up buying my meal.

On another occasion, I was at a conference, and the fellow sitting next to me had ripped jeans and smelled really bad. I thought maybe I could help him out with coaching and began talking to him. Again, I had judged someone by their appearance before finding out the truth about them. It turned out he was helping a friend who lived on a pig farm move and was, in fact, the operations manager for *"Think and Grow Rich!"* Boy, did that ever make me feel humble! I ended up hiring him as a coach for myself and benefitted a lot from his knowledge.

These types of instances prove that it is our inclination to judge others and shows how easily we wrong others in doing so. Feeling that you have been wronged is something that can occupy your mind and consume your thoughts, excluding all else, leading to a serious decline in mental health. Is it any wonder that the indigenous population has such a problem with not only mental health but a lack of trust in the government over all the broken treaties and the recent revelation of all the deaths of children in residential schools? It has come to light also that even such things that the government promised to rectify — like providing clean drinking water for all the reserves who have been under a "Boiled Water Advisory" for twenty years — have still not come to pass. Until we recognize that we have a problem with being judgmental, we will not be able to solve our other mental health issues.

As a therapist, the reality of Covid-19 is that the longer this situation continues, the higher the rate of mental issues climbs. We are seeing this not only in the adult population but also in the youth sector, across all cultures, nationalities, races and socioeconomic groups.

Being the target of unjust judgment is very difficult to overcome and can not only make someone defensive and hostile, but it can also affect relationships and even our general outlook on life. It can cause anxiety, mood changes and can lead to depression, self-injury, obsessions, substance abuse and a host of other disorders.

In an attempt to combat the rise in mental health issues, we each need to adjust not only our perceptions of others but also our actions. This includes making a sincere effort to be aware of how we interact with those around us and how our actions affect them personally. One place to start is examining our own biases and judgmental attitudes and to determine to be more compassionate, less hasty with our criticisms, and be more willing to allow others to express their opinions and concerns. Just feeling that you are heard, can go a long way toward accepting an uncomfortable or unpleasant situation.

Unfortunately, the fact is that people, in general, resist change. Change is uncomfortable and usually is only the result of a crisis in life. For me, it took years of living on the street, in denial that drinking and drugging were ruining any chance of a better life before I came to the conclusion that I not only needed to change — but wanted to change. It took an epiphany of a child at a bus stop saying to her mom, "He needs help." This started the confirmation in my mind and soul that I would change and get the help I needed.

This involved a lot of change, from not only getting clean and sober, which is something that was necessary to start on my road to a new life, but also changing my mindset. This involved the way that I looked at life, including my judgmental attitudes. I am happy to say that eventually, I was able to defeat my negative thoughts and come to a place of acceptance and forgiveness for those that had judged me.

Now that I have been clean and sober for many years, I am able to think a lot more clearly, and a big part of it was studying how 52 of the top achievers in the world were able to achieve their success.

A dear friend of mine from the movie "*The Secret*" said,

> "*There is a law in nature that says, "Any space and time that's not filled with high-priority things will automatically be consumed by low-priority things." So if you don't get up and define how you want your day and how you want your life, then somebody else gets up and defines it for you.*"
> - Dr. John Demartini

The legendary speaker Les Brown said, "*Don't let someone else's opinion of you become your reality.*"

Every successful person has made mistakes in their life, but look at it as a learning curve and they move on. They come from all walks of life, and each with a different outlook on life. However, the one commonality they all share is that they are patient, resilient and resourceful enough to overcome the hurdles and obstacles that may otherwise block their path to success.

Just believe in yourself with your heart, body, and soul and put it out to the universe, and let it happen. It might not be overnight, it might take years, but it is worth it. Every obstacle you overcome gets you one step closer. It took me 15 years to see my overnight success; now, I am starting to live my dream.

Today, I focus on how I can enhance the lives of others and focus on the person I want to be in 10 years, knowing I will never catch up as I will always be chasing myself 10 years ahead. This has allowed me to move forward and overcome a lot of obstacles and achieve massive goals. I am proud of myself, of course, but I know I will never want to be the smartest person in the room, as I still have to learn how others overcome and achieve their success, to help me reach that next level.

"In the end, our lives will be judged not by the things we began, but by the things that our effort and resolve brought to a successful conclusion." – Jim Rohn

Robert J. Moore

Robert J. Moore is a therapist, 5x internationally Awarded Bestseller, Speaker, Business Coach and a publisher with over 100 published books and a recognized publisher with Ingram, working in one of their top programs — Lightning Source. He is a Guinness World Record holder and nominated for "Walk of Fame," won an Honorary Doctorate Degree two times and has impacted the lives of many through the work associated with Magnetic Entrepreneur Inc.

Robert has impacted the lives of over 160,000 people through an emotional tale that has provided insights on how to determine one's worth and create a life worthy of joy and success. Magnetic Entrepreneur Inc.™ is also a publishing company that has published over 100 books all over the world. He is the main publisher for WONM, with 25 of the top doctors in the world.

Robert has impacted the lives of many through the work associated with his International Award-Winning Best-Selling books, "The Better Way Formula – Principles for Success" & Magnetic Entrepreneur. Robert has even co-authored with Jim Rohn's 18-year business partner Kyle Wilson, and world series pitcher Todd Stottlemyre, Les Brown's daughter Serena Brown Travis, Reggie Rusk retired NFL player, Dr. Joe Vitale, from the book and movie "The Secret" etc... Robert has hosted many events with his brand Magnetic Entrepreneur Author Awards, Magnetic Entrepreneur Guinness World Records Attempt, high-end Mastermind, which allow his students to reach the levels they could only dream of.

Robert has been interviewed by magazines from around the world, national TV programs, radio shows, and has also been invited to speak on world-class stages with Jack Canfield, Les Brown, Bob Proctor, Eric Thomas, Douglas Vermeeren and Raymond Aaron.

Robert J. Moore has studied 52 of the top achievers in the world in the past decade to be able to build this amazing program. Robert states that "This is by far one of the greatest works I have ever created. I am honoured to share it with you."

FINDING PEACE AND LOVE — THE SOURCE OF HAPPINESS

Eni Oszlai

Dedicated to Guapo with much love

"When things change inside you, things change around you."
— Unknown

"You, yourself, as much as anybody in the entire universe, deserve your love and affection." — Buddha

When was the last time you looked in the mirror and smiled at the person looking back at you with admiration and appreciation, with love and gratitude, with peace and harmony in your heart?

Why is it easier to live in judgement than to live in harmony?

Are we addicted to suffering?

Since 2004, when I moved to Canada from Cologne, Germany, life has taken many unexpected twists. As a new immigrant, I understood that I needed to restart some aspects of my life – but was not prepared for the deep dive that followed. In Germany, I was managing a multi-billion dollar merger of an international business law firm, globe trotted and enjoyed the high life in my twenties. Then, I followed love and gave up all of this in the hope of a new life with added meaning.

While I was waiting for my immigration papers to come through, I signed up for the business communication certification course of a local college, and also took on my very first job: being a volunteer waitress at a banquet hall, just to obtain that much needed, infamous Canadian work experience. I will never forget the function where we were serving teachers who learned about managing curriculum and classrooms that have children with ADD or ADHD. Having my teacher's diploma from Europe, I was naturally interested in the topic and found it very valuable, and felt fortunate to be exposed to the added knowledge, just by fate's intervention. As we got into a conversation with one of the conference participants, and I said something that struck her attention, she could not help herself but wondered out loud – "So interesting that *you* know about this." Oh well, from her perspective, I was nothing more than a waitress at a banquet hall.

As many other immigrants have experienced, it took several years to get to where I wanted to be. Others will judge – but we decide how we move past it.

Did all those years of building my life back up deter me from going after my goals and vision, and create a life worth living? On the contrary, knowing myself helped me get past the valleys.

As I write this chapter, I am marvelling at humanity and the great collective suffering we choose to embrace and take upon ourselves, not realizing that it leads to the suffering of the animal kingdom, the environment, and even our precious planet, which is in upheaval with unprecedented natural catastrophes. The entire world is still battling the aftermath of a global pandemic and the financial and emotional consequences it brought with it.

As a Financial Doctor, I have the honour and privilege to have deep and meaningful discussions with individuals, families, business people, and even with change-makers and collaborators. As we travel through the deep dive with my clients, they give me their utmost trust to share their life goals and desires, their hopes for themselves and their loved ones, but also their current situation, fears and roadblocks. This gives us the opportunity to start the dream building. Yes, it all starts with a very specific, crystal clear dream!

"If you can dream it, you can do it." — Walt Disney

When we work in a transparent and authentic way to create a road map that can accelerate them on their journey of recovery, they do surpass all of their dreams! The key to this all starts with one very important step: self-discovery, followed by acceptance and self-love.

Many people out there are seemingly fine if you "judge" their situation by their social media posts, but their souls are crying, their lives falling apart. They are losing hope. They choose to numb themselves with ideologies keeping them suffering, or with alcohol and drugs to mask the pain serving as band-aids, without digging deep to the root cause of their inner turmoil.

Haven't we been created in love, in the image of the Creator?

Even if you are not religious, we can agree that there is more to this world than what the naked eye can see. We can't see radio waves or electricity, microwaves or gravity, but we all know they exist – and we benefit from or use them in our everyday lives.

"All religions, arts and sciences are branches of the same tree."
— Albert Einstein

Our Universe is so abundantly rich – and we are all part of it. Our spirits are searching for beauty, peace, harmony and love. Yet, many of us chose to live in fear, guilt and punishment. We all make mistakes, almost every day. So why are we punishing ourselves multiple times for the very same mistake? Why are we even entertaining the idea – I should have, or I should have not … .Why do we "overthink" and second guess our choices so many times? Why do we give away our power by accepting others' judgement over our most sincere actions? Why do we live in fear, believing we are not enough?

When we choose to suffer and live in pain, that is what we radiate out, poisoning our very environment – causing pain and suffering to those we love. By punishing ourselves over and over again, we spread the punishment to others, shutting down the very possibility of living in harmony, joy and happiness.

"If you are depressed, you are living in the past, if you are anxious you are living in the future, if you are at peace, you are living in the present." — Lao Tzu

Many times I hear people saying, "I'll be happy when I get "there" – and they state a specific goal, space or time. Yet, interestingly, once they get there, they are more dissatisfied than ever. Why? Because the joy is in the journey, my friends, every minute of it. It is in the NOW!

"We must be our own before we can be another's." — Ralph Waldo Emerson

Happiness lives in our core. It is us – and only us – who are responsible for going through the journey of self-discovery, self-acceptance and self-love, so that we can be the light for others.

"People think a soul mate is your perfect fit, and that's what everyone wants. But a true soul mate is a mirror, the person who shows you everything that is holding you back, the person who brings you to your own attention so you can change your life." — Elizabeth Gilbert

Guapo is a beautiful soulmate and friend of mine. A true spiritual gem with a BIG heart, filled with kindness, caring for others, wanting to create beauty in and for others. He is someone who survived so much pain yet has grown from it; and while wounded many times over, still creates love and peace for others. It was Guapo who opened my eyes to see beyond borders and limitations I placed upon my life for no other reason but my own fears. That awoke my spirit of wanting and reaching for more, learning and growing more. Yearning to achieve my own wholeness. Guapo broke through invisible walls with sheer kindness and the spirit of an adventurer, and a great teacher who guides his students with patience and love while being open to learning more themselves, too. Growth has followed. And like all growth, it comes with pain and lots of learning, but beauty, harmony and trust, too.

I am enjoying my journey and embracing it. I didn't ask for a grandmaster, but the Universe provided me with it. And we each learn and grow as we walk through the path that is given to us.

It is some of my dearest friends and coaches, the fabulous NLP coach, Linda LeBreton and the lovely spiritual coach, Wilma David, who opened my eyes over the past year and a half that by living in the now, by enjoying every moment, the journey we are on, we can observe so much beauty and harmony, and we can arrive at unconditional love.

"Love is always patient and kind. It is never jealous. Love is never boastful or conceited. It is never rude or selfish. It does not take offense and is not resentful. Love takes no pleasure in other people's sins, but delights in the truth. It is always ready to excuse, to trust, to hope, and to endure whatever comes." — 1 Corinthians 13:4-7

Love is the highest form of vibration and energy in our Universe. Love is never-ending, never leaving, all enduring. Our spirits search for it, and we all want it to flow through our hearts, our minds, our very souls. You can't measure love, but we all feel it. Love is not tangible, something you can force or expect – yet it's a miracle that comes to us, through us – that makes it so much better than as we imagined it. It surprises us in its many forms, uplifts us, and as we give it out, it multiplies. We get it back in waves, multiple folds.

Love is such a beautiful divine emotion and energy. As we accept this heavenly gift that is our birthright, we can't help but realize that we imperfect human beings are perfectly designed to receive and to emit it. Love makes everything and everyone better. Love creates peace and harmony, and unity with the Universe.

"Where there is love there is life." - Mahatma Gandhi.

The Law of Attraction teaches us to manifest good in our lives. Living in Love is living by the Law of Attraction. In fact, it's living by the Laws of Life.

When we live in love, our energy vibrates at a high frequency, and we express the divine qualities of joy, peace, compassion, forgiveness, tolerance, respect, generosity and gratitude. These, in turn, inspire, empower, and enhance life as a whole. When you live in the love vibration, you achieve a higher state of consciousness that frees us of the thoughts, feelings, and actions originating from fear and judgment – feelings that minimize and victimize us.

Imagine a ball that is falling. What does it take for the ball to remain on the floor instead of bouncing back up in the air? However, if there are no imposed blockages, the harder the ball falls, the harder it bounces back up again!

It is our ego that chooses to suffer over our spirit that searches for the love vibration. When we suffer, we are blinded and can't see the truth. When we suffer, we resist Life. However, when you keep your ego in check and allow your spirit to take the lead, you lose the neurotic fear, anger, jealousy, hate, envy, greed, arrogance, guilt – and the need to "be right." Interestingly, once you free yourself from the negative stinking thinking and all its limitations, you can't help but feel lighter and start shining brighter. Suddenly, strangers start smiling at you on the street, opening the doors for you, greeting you, striking up a conversation – and whatever you wish to attract in your life starts showing up for you. You just became the magnet of attracting all the good in your life.

You are creating your own Life! When you find peace, you will find the truth.

"Balance is not something you find, it's something you create." — Jana Kingsford

There are many ways to create that inner harmony and balance. My personal go-to sources are music and nature. I grew up with music, making music, listening to it and absorbing it. Music is part of my fabric, part of who I am. Music gives me the divine joy that raises my vibrations and energy, lifting me up to new heights. My daily nature walks have not only helped to improve my health, but my forest baths serve as an inspiration to reach my equilibrium by becoming one with the Universe.

What are your ways of creating true inner joy in your life?

"Beauty is everywhere. You only have to look to see it." — Bob Ross

Beauty surrounds us in so many ways: in nature, music, poetry and art … and even in people. One of the most beautiful people in my life is my dear friend and soul sister, my business partner: Randi Goodman.

Randi was someone I manifested in my life. A few years ago, when some of my clients met me at events, as I was educating masses about their opportunities to surpass their dreams, but also about financial literacy, empowering my audience to make educated choices, they approached me to connect with Randi Goodman, as she did just the same: provided many platforms for others to spread knowledge and kindness to create greater good for all to enjoy. Randi and I ended up literally bumping into each other at a large networking event – at the coffee station. The rest is history, as they say.

Randi is a major event producer, real estate broker, but also a publisher. She's a mother of four adult sons and someone who is one of the most authentic female warriors I ever met in my life. When the global pandemic shut down the world, negatively affecting individuals, families and business owners, I knew I had to do something more for my clients to uplift them and help them reach a wider audience to attract more clients, but also business partners and collaborators. While my podcast *'The Financial Doctor Show'* became a major success that has been watched and streamed on various platforms for over tens of thousands of times, our collaboration with Randi with the successful *"Empowering Women to Succeed"* international #1 bestselling book series provided an additional, international platform for our authors not only to tell their stories, but to gain an audience and reach beyond borders with their voice – and their business solutions. The positive impact was enormous. I am delighted and grateful to know that we will publish many more books with authors who have the deep desire to inspire and empower others to succeed.

"The more thankful I became, the more my bounty increased. That's because — for sure — what you focus on expands. When you focus on the goodness in life, you create more of it." — Oprah Winfrey

I am grateful for all the learning, the setbacks, the pain, the joy and humility, and all the love and support pouring my way, along with all the beauty surrounding me. I enjoy life, and

I love my journey. No, it's far from being smooth, but it's so rewarding.

"Life isn't about finding yourself. Life is about creating yourself."
— George Bernard Shaw

I invite you to forgive and accept the person who looks back at you from the mirror, to love them for their perfect imperfections, and to live life fully. The inevitable peace, harmony and happiness will follow.

With Love and Gratitude,

Your Musical Financial Doctor: Eni Oszlai

Eni Oszlai

Eni Oszlai is an Award-winning Financial Doctor, RBC's TOP Financial Specialist in Canada. She holds several financial licences, a Masters in Adult Education, and has completed the coaching program based on Bob Proctor's *'Law of Attraction.'* Eni believes in continuous improvement and personal growth, and since 2020, she has also been mastering Tony Robbins' NLP program with her own coach. She's an expert in helping her clients make their dreams and vision a tangible reality!

Eni is a leading activist with Global Citizen eradicating worldwide poverty, combatting human trafficking and worldwide pollution, and fighting for humanitarian and environmental issues.

She is also a music lover and connoisseur. Eni helps artists uncover their true potential, be featured on media, and increase their follower base.

Her Podcast, the *"Financial Doctor Show,"* has attracted and featured musicians and business owners, change-makers and trailblazers: a TEDx Speaker, a Social Media Correspondent for the OSCARS and Golden Globes, an Order of Canada Recipient, and a former MP. Her three international bestselling books are: *"The Waterfront Awards: Powerful Success Stories"* (2020), and *"Empowering Women to Succeed: Legacy"* (2021), and *"Women of Inspiration ™: Women Driving Change"* (2021).

Eni is the co-publisher of the 6-time international bestselling series *"Empowering Women to Succeed,"* propelling individuals, business owners and speakers to new heights never experienced before.

Eni is truly building a Legacy by Empowering others to Succeed!

https://www.enioszlai.com/
https://www.empoweringwomentosucceed.com/
416-543-6127

DON'T JUDGE

Marianne Padjan

Have you ever met someone, and because they have tattoos all over their body, thought to yourself, "Why is it that I'm a little afraid of this person?"

Perhaps it wasn't a tattooed person, and maybe they were overweight, but you thought to yourself, "Why they must be really lazy," or maybe they were wearing glasses, and you thought, "Wow, for sure they are super smart!"

Isn't it interesting how we make judgments on the basis of a first glance? This means that that means this.

Life is funny and full of assumptions that we have created as a result of our past and then also mostly based on other people's opinions. What would this world look like if we just accepted everyone for who they are and made decisions on what we think of people once we got to know them?

What if we actually gave people a chance to show us who they Are. Wouldn't it be great if we just accepted them for who they are?

Why is it so hard to be authentic, and why are we so scared of it? Wouldn't it just be easier if we could all be ourselves? If you've ever been around someone who is almost 100% themselves, it's just so much easier to be around them. Everything kind of flows, and it feels like you're in a river of easy-breezy energy. It's when we feel like we have to act like someone else that we just absolutely mess everything up. Everything gets intense; you must keep up with your own lies because you're trying to pretend to be someone or something that you're not. It makes it more emotional, it creates drama, and it creates chaos all around for everyone involved, not just the person who's doing it but everyone who's within that person's energy. It makes you want to just walk away.

It's hard to be friends with someone like that, and it's almost impossible to do business with them because they don't know if they're coming or going. That energy reflects itself in their behaviour, and then you can't do anything with that, you're stuck, you're both stuck, or all of you in the whole group are stuck because everyone's trying to be something they're not, and it doesn't work that way.

We were never meant to be someone else. God made us the way we are, and this is who we should accept being and enjoy it, and make the best of all that we are.

So, when someone actually is themselves, should we really judge them before we get a chance to know them? I mean, I used to work in retail many years ago, and I had a boss that always used to judge people who walked in by, "Oh, they have lots of money," or "They don't." So if they don't have lots of money, don't give them the time of day, but if they do, spend lots of time speaking with them. Well, one time, there was a young lady who walked in, and she had a baseball cap on, and she was wearing jeans. She was wearing plain clothing, but you could tell it was all fairly high-end clothing. Not that any of that mattered, I would speak to anyone anyway. I figured, you're in the store, and you're going to be buying something, and my job is to help serve you. Well, it turned out that she was quite the millionaire, and she ended up buying quite a bit. It was back maybe 30 years ago. She spent just over $1000 in our jean store, which was a lot back then. Had I chosen to judge her somehow by her clothing, as my boss did, I think things would have gone differently for me that day.

In my life, I have been in many situations such as that. Not only am I more intrigued with the person that doesn't look like they belong, but I end up talking to them almost the better part of the evening if I'm at a party, a business event or at a networking event. You never know who is going to capture your attention and with whom you will make a better connection, and perhaps even a lifelong relationship may develop.

The other thing I have found very interesting in the way that karma and energy work is that if you judge people by their "cover," people will, in turn, judge you by your cover. Let's face it, every single day that I go to the grocery store, I do not get all dressed up with makeup and my hair done. But it also does not mean that I am, by any means, a hot mess every day. I prefer not to be judged and, therefore, will do my best not to judge others at all!

I focus on looking at all of us as GOD'S CHILDREN. We are all humans with a variety of issues and values and could look at others as an extension of ourselves. While we are all different, we are all very much the same! We really are brothers and sisters in the grand picture of life!

PEACE AND LOVE

Marianne Padjan

Marianne finds people fascinating and is passionate about empowering and inspiring them. The learning part for her never ever ends as she has been taking courses and has used a variety of coaches for the past 30 plus years. She is a bit of a COURSE JUNKIE! Marianne is also an international award-winning, bestselling author, Guinness World Record Holder and Participant, an Empowerment Coach, Workshop Facilitator, Retreat Leader, Ordained Minister, Award Winner with International Forum for Advancement in Healthcare, Reiki Master, Meditation Specialist, Kundalini Yoga teacher, a Real Estate Agent with EXP Realty and soon to be a DIGITAL TV host. That is definitely an eclectic variety that keeps her busy! She is happy to say that she has impacted many lives both professionally as well as personally. She has guided them from divorce to marriage as well as from bankruptcy to millionaire status. She enjoys engaging people in their own growth so they find their power again and thrive! She will help you recognize your GREATNESS, find your authenticity and help you to achieve your dreams!

Email: Spiritualtouch11@gmail.com

Facebook: marianne padjan@facebook.com

BEFORE JUDGING - FIND OUT SOMEONE'S STORY

Alan Wade

I know that I have been judged by others for years. As a teenager, I had long hair, and people would judge me by that look. Yes, I did fall into the world of drugs and alcohol, or I should say I jumped into the world of darkness. I remember asking girls to go out with me, and I'd hear on a few different occasions, "I do not date long-haired hippies." Even today, I still have people judge me as soon as they see me. Yes, I still have the long hair, and I am a very relaxed dresser. So you would think after experiencing people judge me by my looks that I would not do it to someone else.

As a teenager and even into my late twenties, I was not a very happy person. In fact, I was very mean, hurtful, rude, and any other words you can find to describe someone that was selfish. I was struggling with a very traumatic event that happened to me when I was ten years old. I justified my actions and even hurt people because I felt entitled to hurt others because I was hurt. I share this with you due to a person I judged when I was around eighteen years old and into my early twenties. I have never told this to anyone else. It is embarrassing just to be rethinking it, but it is also a very powerful lesson I would use to see the world differently years later.

There was this older man in the area I lived, probably a few years older than I was. He dressed very colourfully. He appeared happy all the time, singing as he walked, and really I can honestly say I saw him do anything mean or wrong to anyone. I would tease him when I saw him walking down the street. I was rude, never violent, but very rude. It was all because of the way he dressed and acted.

At the age of twenty-seven, I started the process of changing my life around. I let go of my unhealthy attitudes and learned even to let go of my anger. It would be years later when I would run into this person again, and by this time, I was in a much better place. I remember sitting in a park in the town I lived. There he was, sitting on a bench; immediately, I felt this wave of guilt come over me. I suddenly remembered how I was rude to him. As I sat there, I remember this fear come over me as well, and I remember getting up to leave the area. I am not sure why or what came over me, but I turned around and went to talk with him.

I told him who I was and what I had done to him in my earlier years and apologized. As I was speaking with him, I felt shame, guilt, embarrassment and even anger at myself. When I was finished, he looked at me and said he did not remember me. He did go on to say that apparently, I was not the only one that teased him. In fact, he stated that he was beaten up many times. As we talked more, I found out that he was a regular in the park and knew many people there.

As I got to know him better over time, he shared with me that he struggled with a mental illness, and when he would walk down the street when he was younger, the singing helped him deal with the voices in his head. I felt this sick feeling come over me. I just remembered all the names I had called him. Here I was teasing a man who was struggling with schizophrenia. There was no excuses for how I treated him or how I judged him. The amazing thing was I think he saw my reaction when he told me about his illness, and he was very understanding. He said that, "In the early years, doctors had very little knowledge of the illness." Here was this very forgiving and understanding man dealing with a serious illness telling me, "It is okay." We did become friends.

He told me about people in the park and their struggles. Why I share this with you is I actually had an opportunity to share something I learned with the clients of the addictions and rehabilitation program. A life lesson I remember to this day.

One day, I overheard people speaking negatively about the older gentleman being drunk and passed out on the sidewalk. They were saying negative things about him, such as, "Look at him; he is pathetic." I remember feeling that sick feeling I had when I thought about teasing that man all those years ago. The man who would later become my friend and teach me so much about things I knew very little about.

What happened next was amazing. I was able to use what the people were saying negatively about the older man as a teaching moment. I asked them why they were speaking negatively about the man. Some replied, "He is a bum getting drunk all the time." Someone else mentioned, "He always asks for money." "Look at him he is passed out on the sidewalk." That is when I asked, "Does anyone know his story?" We all have a story I said; "I have one, you have one," and "Does anyone know his?" I asked again." "No" is what I got.

So I began to share with them my story of how I judged a person when I was young just from the way he looked and acted. They were surprised, and some said, "Really?" I went on to tell them how I met him in the park years later and how I apologized, and he forgave me, and we actually became friends. What was amazing was he had introduced me to the older gentleman.

That is how I had found out that the person they were calling a bum was not always that way. That, in fact, he was a respected professor at a university. He made great money, had a big house, fancy car, and a wife and daughter. Then, one day there was a terrible car accident, and his wife and daughter were killed in the accident.

That, in fact, that man would go on to lose everything he had worked his whole life for in a freak accident. He never was able to return to work, lost his job, lost his home and cars; in fact, he lost himself. How he left the city he lived in and ended up on the streets of the town we lived in. I could see that some of the clients I was speaking with were emotional about his story.

What happened next was really amazing. From time to time, I would catch the clients helping out the elderly gentleman. They would share smokes with him and even some money at times. They would even sneak some food out of the program to give to him. These clients were not rich at all; it was amazing to see them helping someone they really just met.

The lesson learned from this whole experience is not to judge a book by its cover. Do I still get judged by people? Yes, I do, but these days I do not let what others think of me affect me. Today I keep this very valuable lesson with me at all times. As someone that works with very disadvantaged people, it helps me not to come to any conclusions about what other people are or even what they have been through.

Alan Wade

Alan Wade is a Guinness World Record participant, four-time International Best Selling Author, Founder and coach at The Magic Within Coaching and Consulting Company, Certified Master Practitioner of "NLP" Neuro-Linguistic Programming, Certified Hypnotherapy "MER®," Mental Emotion Release. The Magic Within Coaching uses cutting-edge, non-invasive techniques and integrative coaching to help clients release negative emotions attached to traumatic events as well as limiting beliefs. Alan has worked in the field of Addiction and Mental Health for over ten years. He is also the founder of The Magic Within Book Series.

Alan can be reached at: 705 698 2437

tmwbookseries@gmail.com
https://www.facebook.com/alan.wade.921
https://www.instagram.com/themagic.within
Website: themagicwithinseries.com

A Second Look

Dr. Catharina Aletta Lindeque Hunter (Ph.D., IMD, DNM, DHS, DPSc)

"We and God have business with each other and opening ourselves to His influence, our deepest destiny is fulfilled." ~ William James

Do you think book covers, in general, do a good job of enticing readers and giving them an idea of what the book is about? Why would people tell you not to judge a book by its cover? These sayings are idioms. They mean you shouldn't judge the value or worth of something or someone based solely upon outward appearances. In life, in general, this is good advice. Appearances can be deceiving. Before you can make a judgment about something's value or worth, you need to take the time to investigate it fully. Take a deeper, closer look. You might be surprised by what you find. True worth and value aren't always obvious when we only look at the surface.

Imagine this; you are out shopping, and decide to sit down and have a refreshing drink at this cute little restaurant that allows you to sit outside on the patio, while browsing the menu for something healthy to snack on. A person walking by that's heavily obese catches your eye; she is dressed nicely at first glance, her hair and make-up are done, and she looks good, and you are rejoicing for her for taking care of herself. As you are looking at her, you realize her top is creeping up, and her wobbly white stomach is showing more of itself; you are now fascinated. Then you take a second look and realize the top is made of mesh, and all she has on underneath it is a lace bra, and suddenly you are repulsed. How could she be so cruel to herself? How could she shame herself like this in public? How can they make jeans that size? Why has no one told her she shouldn't be wearing that in public? Maybe she should consider eating less and poop more. All these thoughts are flooding your mind.

Or perhaps you meet someone, and you make an instant connection with them; you feel safe and just know they're authentic and kind. You go home and tell your friends and family you met this awesome person, and you are considering bringing them into an area of your life that you need support in. You and your friends or family immediately start researching this person and find some things said on the internet that aren't at all what you observed and felt the person presented themselves as. You are confused, upset, and don't know what is going on. You now have a few choices; you can either ask this person about the information you found online and get their side of the story so you can make a decision if you want to engage in a relationship. You can simply believe what is online, because you can't trust people nowadays and walk away, just to find out later that this person was in fact who you thought they were when you met them, and what was said online was an act of maliciousness.

Or perhaps you are the one that is being blamed and shamed or humiliated. Maybe you did it; maybe you did not. Should your life be forever stuck in that moment, and you and everything you have done in your life up to that point, and then after that be defined through that moment?

Has this ever happened to you? If you say no, this chapter is not for you. If you are able to say yes, I recognize this scenario — or something similar to this, then I would like to invite you to read on and to choose to receive maximum value in this chapter, by being engaged, open to the process, being honest with yourself, taking your biggest risk, and to trust yourself. The person that gave you this book, if it was a gift, and I would like you to trust me as you go through this chapter.

How We Judge

"Our deepest fear is not that we are inadequate. Our deepest fear is that we are powerful beyond measure. It is our light, not our darkness, that most frightens us. We ask ourselves, who am I to be brilliant, gorgeous, talented, and fabulous? Actually, who are you not to be? Your playing small does not serve the world. There is nothing enlightened about shrinking so that other people will not feel insecure around you. We are all meant to shine. We were born to make manifest the glory of God that is within us, and it is not just in the special ones; it is in everyone. As we let our light shine brightly, we unconsciously give others permission to do the same. As we are liberated from fear, our presence automatically liberates others." ~ Marianne Williamson

Have you noticed how quickly you judge and the reasons why? Most of the time, we judge so quickly we don't even realize that we are judging; we have been conditioned to think we are merely making decisions based on the information we have. Well, where is this information coming from? What if you have the wrong information? What if, instead, we decide to notice and become aware of the internal processing and how our body reacts to the external stimuli? What if we decide that something is not right or wrong, and instead, we just choose to notice what happens. Do you feel a resistance in your body? I bet you that you do. What thoughts were you having? Did you notice that more of the same thoughts came?

Have you noticed how you feel when you are around someone that is constantly judging other people? You probably feel less energized and even become prone to judging yourself and other people more. This is because we are energetic light bodies. Frequency affects us in a huge way, causing geopathic stress that can eventually cause us to become sick.

What if we decide to take responsibility for every decision we make, whether it is a good one or a bad one? What if, instead, we decide not to judge ourselves, other people or a situation that turned out not to be the best thing ever? Wecan say, "So what, I made a decision, it is not good or bad, it just is." When have we decided that taking responsibility is equal to fault or failure? Get this, 99% of our decisions are made by our programs. Are you living your best life now? If not, consider that you are running some programs that are not currently serving you. Maybe they did a long time ago because you needed to survive through a traumatic situation, and now today, you struggle to trust people and yourself as a result of that. What are you committed to creating in your life? Here is the thing, change is the one thing we can all be sure of in this world, and it's not good, it's not bad, it just is. If you are not committed to intentionally create the change in your life, something will create the change for you. What if you chose to suspend judgment and just notice? Do you think you would have more possibility to create the change you want in your life; your relationships, your finances, your health, etc.?

To BE, To Listen...

"Whatever we plant in our subconscious mind and nourish with repetition and emotion will one day become a reality." ~ Earl Nightingale

We choose… to be, or to react; thus choosing to be a victim or to be responsible and present. Let me explain. Imagine you are sitting across from a man, having a very sincere and open conversation and he tells you his most traumatic story, " My brother that I was very close to (we did almost everything together), was murdered in front of his wife, on the beach by gang members initiating a new member. I was supposed to go fishing with them, and I was running late. I blame myself for him dying because if I had been there, I could have protected him, and he wouldn't have died. It's my fault. Would you say his man's story made you feel empathetic toward him and the loss he experienced? I am pretty sure you felt his emotions of loss and pain. Do you believe that he could have suffered a tremendous loss and have been a victim in this traumatic moment? Absolutely. Do you know that this man lost almost everything that was important to him in the next two years after that and became an alcoholic?

How did things change for him? Things didn't change for him until he changed his mind and chose to take his power back. He chose to stop giving his power to the situation. How do we do that? We create the change by choosing and leaning into our new choice, choosing to Be. Let me explain. We can take the same scenario; from a place of taking responsibility – taking our power back. For example, "My brother, that I was very close to (we did almost everything together), was murdered in front of his wife, on the beach by gang members initiating a new member. The plan was to go fishing with him and his wife, and I chose to be late - making my business a priority. I was unable to protect him and his wife at the time of his murder. I was still working when I chose to answer the call when I was told that he was murdered. I chose to drive directly to the scene. When the police needed someone to identify the body, I chose to identify the body, taking the stress off my family, and so that I could have a few final moments with him." Would you say his man's story made you feel empathetic toward him and the loss he experienced? I am pretty sure you felt his emotions of loss and pain. Do you believe that he could have suffered a tremendous loss? Absolutely. Do you feel a new power? Do you maybe feel the change in energy? Absolutely, he was even able to see afterward how he was actually helping his family through the process and that he was an invaluable part of their journey in recovering from that traumatic event.

Exercise:

Write down your victim story.
Victim story:

_____

_____

_____.

Responsible Story:

_____

_____

_____.

(Make sure you have the words I chose/ I choose in there as part of taking responsibility and taking your power back. For most people, this will immediately be empowering.)

How do you move to confidence when all you see is shame? How do you carry shame when it's not your truth? You choose … you look at the facts, and write them down. Then on the right side of the fact, write the meaning that you gave to the facts. Now that we have looked at the facts and the meaning we gave it, what if we say that it's not right or wrong, it just is. We can now ask, "Is this still serving me?" If the answer is no, change it. If the answer is yes, can we improve it?

Eg.

Fact	Meaning
My brother was murdered, and I wasn't there…	I failed my brother and my family; I wasn't there when they needed me, I am a failure. Why bother with life? Anyway, I suck; I should have died - not my brother. I lost everything that mattered when he died. I am useless; I couldn't even arrive on time, I don't deserve anything, life sucks, etc.

Can you see how the meaning he gave to the fact that happened changed the course of his life and in two years, he wasn't really speaking with his family? He lost his fiancé, his son, his home and everything he had worked for. He was either getting drunk or fishing and working just enough to keep his fishing and drinking habits going. He became rude and distant to the people that loved and cared for him.

On a separate page, physically write out the following:

Rewrite the fact and attach a new meaning that would serve you once you have chosen to take responsibility. (Look at your responsible story, write the fact again and choose a new meaning that would serve you again.)

Eg.

Fact	Meaning
My brother was murdered, and I wasn't there …	I am an integral part of my family's recovery; my brother died loving his family well, he was a great brother to me, and I was a great brother to him. I have tremendous value, I have fond memories of the times we had together. I am alive and live well every day, etc.

Great Job! Now go ahead and tear up, burn or delete the 1st fact/meaning sheet you made. Now speak the second page's words over yourself every day in front of a mirror.

Within weeks of taking responsibility for himself and choosing to take his power back, creating a new positive meaning that would serve him best now and moving forward, the gentleman in the example's business suddenly took off and he met a woman that then became his wife. He restored his relationship with his parents and quit drinking altogether. His life is very different than what it was then. Does the fact still remain that his brother was murdered? Yes, but his mindset changed and with it, his beliefs that were creating his reality.

To judge, or not to…

It is not what you went through, but how you grow through it that matters most. Surround yourself with people that will be your "source of water." If they don't water you, and you don't water them, you need new people around you. Don't take criticism from people that "don't dare greatly," that won't join you "in the arena" – they sit and watch and have a lot to say, but won't be courageous and vulnerable. Don't wait for other people's belief systems about your life and circumstances to line up with yours before you start believing in yourself. You choose to be significant in your own life, and they will follow. You change the meaning of the facts that you have given these situations, decide what the prices and benefits (risk/rewards) are and if it is worth it, and live your best life now!

Love yourself enough to eat high-frequency foods, drink high-frequency water and juices, mix with people that are living a high-frequency life, choose higher vibrational emotions and see yourself soar! Each morning when you take your head off your pillow, know that you have everything you need.

Disclaimer:

The information, including but not limited to text, graphics, images, and other material contained in this chapter, is for informational purposes only. It is not intended to be a substitute for professional medical advice, diagnosis or treatment. Always seek the advice of your physician or other qualified health care provider with any questions you may have regarding a medical condition or treatment and before undertaking a new health care regimen, and never disregard professional medical advice or delay in seeking it because of something you have read.

Catharina A. Hunter

Catharina A. Hunter is a Board Certified Doctor of Integrative Medicine and a Board Certified Alternative Medical Practitioner who is globally recognized for her expertise in Naturopathic Oncology, Energy Medicine, Chronic Disease Prevention, Behavioral Neurology, and Integrative Medicine Modalities. She is also a Vitalist Associate of the Naturopathic Institute, a Diplomat for Pastoral Science, and a Holistic Health Practitioner.

Catharina is a published author, speaker and educator committed to training professionals and laymen in holistic, integrative medicine, including serving as a professor and dissertation mentor at the International University of Integrative Medicine and the Integrative Quantum Health Institute. She is the founder of Integrative Quantum Health Institute LLC and currently serves as CEO of her clinic in Texas and as a researching Physician with PhotonX Holdings.

For more information, you can contact her on www.iquisa.com or email her at drchunter@protonmail.com

WHAT THE HECK, UNCLE SPECK?

Laura Mae Jones

On many occasions, Mom would say, "Laura Mae, you have champagne taste on a beer budget — You better wish in one hand and crap in the other and see which one gets filled faster!"

Although having an eye and appreciation for the finer things in life, my parents' divorce when I was age seven resulted in being raised in poverty until I became a teenager in high school.

If money were earned by one's devotion, dedication and wholehearted passion for helping others, being raised by a single parent of six would not have been a struggle whatsoever.

Mom, also known as Savilla M. Penrose, RN, worked at Pennhurst Mental Asylum in Spring City, Pennsylvania, during the 1960s until it was shut down by the Government for the horrid conditions and abuse that had been going on for many years.

In charge of 75 homicidal and suicidal patients, Mom was locked in behind closed doors with two orderlies and two nurses aides for each shift. She would share the horrors she had seen daily, the abandoned children that were placed there by their families for things such as epilepsy or for being deaf. They were society's "shame," and they were hidden away, abandoned, tortured and even lobotomized in extreme cases.

Having witnessed patients on Mom's ward that were handcuffed to their metal crib because they would injure themselves severely if they were not restrained, together with patients who had to wear helmets or they would bite off ears, noses or harm themselves severely, kept me constantly frightened for my Mom's safety, for the patients' safety, and for the suffering in their eyes. It was the profound expression of the deepest loneliness resulting from being unloved, abandoned and left behind. They were alone, an empty shell. They truly had little to look forward to, and I wondered how they could survive.

I never wanted to be abandoned and alone. This created the people-pleaser attitude I had. I wanted to be loved, to belong and to make my family proud, even my dad. If my dad couldn't love me, I must be unlovable became my core belief. He was the first to abandon me at age seven.

My oldest sister was born in 1947 at six months, weighing less than two pounds. There was no neonatal care in those days. Dianne Marie was expected to be hopelessly retarded and would need to be institutionalized. Mom proved them wrong. I knew if Mom would never institutionalize her child at the strong suggestion of the doctors, I certainly would never be abandoned like that. I was wrong.

I remember my Sunday rides with Dad to go pick Mom up at Pennhurst after her shift. The grounds seemed massive to me, like a compound of brick buildings, barred windows and people gazing hopelessly outdoors with no chance of ever getting to leave that tragic place. It made my heart hurt to think about it.

The higher functioning patients would be walking on the grounds. However, they were nothing compared to any of the people I saw walking off of those grounds. Again, it frightened me. I prayed for those people every night. I didn't understand how God could make such a mistake. They were still human beings without hope. I prayed for their healing anyway.

Mom was no stranger to caring for others. Her Mother, Hannah Mae Penrose, was a midwife and nurse. She would deliver babies at my Mom's childhood home. At times, the babies wouldn't survive, and Mom would rock the baby until the coroner arrived. Mom was very young and relieved her own heartache by playing her baby grand piano. She was playing Mozart at age four.

Being a Penrose descendant from The House of Windsor in England, Mom was used to a lavish lifestyle at such a young age. However, when the stock market crashed in 1929, all of their money was gone. There would be no more luxuries. My grandfather was unable to adjust to rations, hunger, and fell into a state of mental trauma, and later died of angina caused by acute anxiety.

The Penrose family was a family of remarkably high standards. All my Grandpa's uncles graduated from Harvard. They were doctors, Senators (Senator Boyce Penrose), Brigadier General Arthur Penrose, and one black sheep, Uncle Spencer Penrose, who had been disowned and disinherited for being on the "wild side" and who had barely graduated Harvard with a bachelor's degree.

He was an extreme prohibitionist for alcohol and was no stranger to gambling or risky endeavours. He was sent away. I never heard more about him other than that Mom received money from him every year for her birthday until she was 15.

It was in 1994; we found out that was the time of his passing. She never knew where he went or what had happened to him. Families did not discuss things like that back then.

My grandfather, Edward Boyce Penrose, was an accountant for the railroad and a mortician. Mom recounted the highlight of Grandpa's life was the annual trip via railroad that he and my grandma would take to Colorado. They always stayed at the Brown Palace Hotel on Tremont Street in Denver, Colorado.

It was not until decades later, in 1994, that the truth unfolded in front of Mom's eyes on the cover of The Denver Post that revealed a family secret that even she was kept in the dark about until that wonderful day. It turned out that Uncle Spencer had become a successful entrepreneur and philanthropist. He made his fortune from mining, ore processing, and real estate speculation in Colorado and other parts of the West. He founded the Utah Copper Company in 1903 and also established mining operations in Arizona, New Mexico and Nevada.

My favourite memory of my childhood was the month-long visits we would have with my grandmother, Hannah Mae Penrose, each summer. We ate orange sherbet every night, and she would tell me endless stories of her life. It was those stories that explained to me how I got that champagne taste on a beer budget. It was from her, my mother and my ancestors.

We never give much thought to meeting ancestors or whether they watch over us. We do not give much thought to the traits we may have inherited from ancestors beyond our parents and grandparents. In 2015, after a near-death experience, I realized I, too, was destined for greatness like Uncle Speck. I was not destined to be worthless, unloved, unwanted, abandoned, not good enough. I was determined to give hope to the world, the entire hurting world, with loving-kindness, love and light.

Before you can shine your inner light, you must come out of the darkness. The Lord knows how desperately I sought for the way out of my darkness.

Having travelled the mental health system consistently for 30 years, receiving many, many medications and therapy sessions only left me paralyzed and stuck in that darkness for over 50 years.

Everyone gave up on me and, at last, gave up on myself.

On September 29, 2015, I ingested a bottle of my husband's heart medication and woke up on life support three days later.

While in a coma, I had a near-death experience that changed and transformed all that I was into all that I am now. I was in heaven's womb.

At first, I thought I was in purgatory or a holding place. I had no fear or panic. All of my love and memories were with me. I was swaddled in the most abundant love, and my God was on my left side. I received a knowing of many things, an understanding and gift of creativity I never had prior to that day. Six years later, I continue to receive God's downloads to my soul.

All things are possible through our God of mercy and amazing grace and glory.

Mindfulness is the cure for preventing mental illness and the only way to overcome the bondage of depression and anxiety

If there is one thing I am certain of, and that is we want the same things. We want to become the highest form of ourselves, to be better today than we were yesterday, to make the world a better place with loving-kindness and compassion.

I could not have foreseen the true impact that a deceased ancestor would have on my recovery later in life. The more I learned about Spencer's life; a fire lit inside of me that manifested a completely different mindset relating to my self worth as a human being, my future potential, and the courage to be vulnerable enough to step into my potential through self-love and the confidence to speak my truth.

It is because of Uncle Speck's legacy that I was inspired to build myself from the grave to greatness. On September 29, 2015, I was on life support. On September 4, 2021, I received a Lifetime Achievement Award for my contribution to "Nation Building, Social Welfare and Education." The

Award states that MY LIFE has lightened the path of many and will ALWAYS guide the coming generation.

Respectfully submitted with loving-kindness,

Laura Mae Jones, North Carolina

Laura Mae Jones

Laura Mae Jones is a Mindfulness Master, Paralegal, Notary Public, Author, International Motivational Speaker, Artist, Empowerment Model and is passionate about affecting mental health reform by teaching Mindfulness.

Additionally, she is the proud wife of John W. Jones, Retired Master Sergeant, United States Marine Corps, a disabled veteran who served 30 years.

In addition, she is a joyful mother, grandmother and great grandmother.

It is her hope to be a ripple of love, hope and light to the world.

Having been on life support in 2015 and having a near-death spiritual experience, she is a true living testimony that we are all one created by God

Her message is to spread love and kindness globally and to pass her wisdom to all those seeking to create a life of inner peace, self-love, compassion for others, and to make every moment count.

https://www.facebook.com/mindfulnessmaster

WhatsApp: 19104415814831usa

THE VOICE

HM Dr. Uba Iwunwa

It was a very hot summer afternoon on July 12, 2020, when I arrived at the Ottawa International Airport in Canada for the "All Nations International Women's Convention." I was very excited to see a few women who came for the conference at the designated meeting point at the airport arrival spot for a shuttle bus to the hotel.

There was this unpleasant lady that caught my attention in a negative way. She looked out of place and kept walking around and introducing herself to people as Dr. Beena. At first, I thought that she was a panhandler but later noticed that she came for the conference.

Looking at her from head to toe, I wondered why such a person would not crawl into a hole and hide. Instead, she chose to be the center of attention. You could see the startled looks on everybody's faces as this strange woman kept on talking loudly to the four women sitting beside her.

She was dressed in an old pair of jeans with a very old yellow-flowered boyish cowboy shirt. She covered her hair with a purple bandana; what a weird way to dress, I said to myself. Her outfit looked so ancient, but she couldn't care less and was full of energy.

Just being around this woman made me anxious. A few people walked away to distance themselves from her loud annoying voice, but I was curious to know the reason why the people close to her seemed to be very interested in whatever she was saying to them. And what gave her the audacity to be such a monopolizer of the conversation? I drew closer when she said, "There comes a time in someone's life when you have to look back at the past and be grateful for every one of life's bitter challenges that have caused you to fight for your destiny to live life from your true authentic self." I stopped to look at her properly and just wondered about the meaning of this 'authentic self' based on her appearance. Then the host of the conference arrived, and we all entered the shuttle bus to the hotel. This strange woman continued talking. At the hotel, we were briefed by the host, who welcomed each of us with a conference package, and I rushed to my room to get ready for the evening program but was saddened with a mere thought that this so-called Dr. Beena would ruin the whole weekend.

A tall, beautifully dressed lady walked up on the stage at the women's empowerment program that evening. Her beautiful flowing curly long red hair took my breath away. Her smoky eye makeup made her face look like a goddess of Egypt. She picked up the microphone and introduced herself as Dr. Beena Ezenna. Dr. Beena? I choked on my own saliva, my eyes blinked. How could that be? Angels do show up in different forms. What a transformation, the same talkative annoying ugly lady from the airport? My whole body began to shiver from shock as most people turned to each other in surprise and shock. Dr. Beena majestically walked close to the edge of the stage as if she knew our dilemma and cleared her throat. The whole hall was dead silent; you could hear a pin drop.

In what seemed like a soliloquy, she began to speak to a hall filled with women of all nations in a very harmonious voice, crystal clear like a sweet melody. She said, "At the dawn of awakening, life seems like an oyster, the shell may not be pretty, it has been beaten by nature, but inside of that ugly looking thing is a beautiful precious pearl. I laid down my life because my soul knew that it was part of my creator's plan. The greatest failure is an unfulfilled destiny. Each and every one of us came into this world with a purpose ordained by our creator. Take a look in the mirror and ask yourself, 'Am I walking the path of my destiny or am I pursuing someone else's dream, vision and purpose out of jealousy and envy?' Many chase after anything just to compete. When you waste your life chasing after other people's success, your own destiny is left undone. You may achieve wealth, fame and power, but you will surely end your life with an unfinished and unfulfilled destiny." She looked around in silence, and she continued.

"Failure starts the moment you allow factors of life to define who you are and hold you down. On the judgement day, everyone will answer for himself or herself. That child, mother, father, brother, sister, uncle, auntie, niece, nephew, friend, and well-wishers that cause you not to fulfill your destiny will never answer for you or be an excuse for your failure. The only person who failed to achieve your purpose is you, not circumstances. Everyone lives and answers for themselves. Life factors are mere obstacles set on your path to break you, test you, block you and derail you from your purpose. The battle of destiny must cost you to be worth it. Despite what's set on your path, choose to conquer the world; never allow the world to conquer you. Blessings come with the price of obedience; obedience is costly, but the end result is always priceless. Everyone runs after success, but no one tries to duplicate the solid foundation for it. Before you judge a person or envy their success, have you walked in their shoes and travelled on the road that led them to where they are today? No matter your circumstances today, embrace them with gratitude and believe that it's only a process, not a life sentence. Remember, the greater your storm, the brighter your rainbow." She nodded.

With a smile and a loud voice, she said, "Hope will no longer be silenced. The time is now to release what no longer serves you. Follow your intuition and stop feeling lost or damaged. The wind of change is blowing on you; it blows forward, and there's no turning back from here now. From this mutual point of interest, may the Universe grant us balance and equality to align to our higher soul's purpose. No more will our past hold us hostage. That circle has ended the moment you allowed your authentic self to answer this call; this is a clarion call to remove the ugly garment of your past."

She pulled back and placed the microphone on its stand, and she put her palms together in a praying mode. "I may fail you today. I may have failed my family, friends and well-wishers, but my final destination is never to fail on my purpose on earth. I came to this world with an ordinance of God, not man. I owe my creator the accountability for what He placed in my life, not who the world wants me to be. Life begins the moment you realize your purpose on earth. Never live your life to please anyone; live for the fulfillment of your destiny." She smiled with great confidence.

"The battle of destiny is not about those who reject you, mock you, slander you, and oppress you but your courage, endurance, faith and tenacity to finish your race. No matter your pain and suffering along life's journey, always remember that your creator is waiting for you at the finish line." She lifted her eyes and looked up as if God was there, and she whispered, "Abba Father, I surrender to your will." She held the microphone and looked at the crowd. "No apology for who I am or the path that I have surrendered my life to tread upon. Never join the rat race; find your true life calling. Declare your purpose, embrace it and own it. That tiny voice within you is asking you to live your life from your authentic self; the blueprint of your creator is within you. Your victory lies in your courage to fight the good fight. A mirror never loses its ability to reflect, even if it is broken into two or a thousand pieces. The time has come for you to become the higher expression of yourself and start living your life from your authentic self by allowing your inner beauty to take center stage. Beloved, say out loud, 'I am who God says I am.' Thank you all, and God bless."

Everyone started clapping and yelling with excitement and gratitude for such a wonderful speech. I froze in my seat because her speech hit home. I've been a shell of myself, not having the courage to speak my own truth of who I am. Dr. Beena became a wake-up call and a voice of reason. I was completely glued to my seat while everyone left the hall. I sat there in silence as tears filled my eyes. Tears of pain and regret for how long I'd lived only to please others. I had tears for the missed opportunity of meeting her one-on-one at the airport when I had the chance. Then the hall became dark, and someone closed the door without realizing that I was still sitting there drowning in my own self-pity and self-realization of the true meaning of living life from your authentic self. Who would have thought that the same dreadful, haggard-looking lady from the airport was the most beautiful and amazing woman in that hall that evening and the key speaker of the convention. She is a woman with a golden voice, an international, multiple award-winning motivational speaker — a #1 international bestselling author of several books. I desperately needed another chance to meet her. Meeting her was the reason for the conference, but this time, I would have to book an appointment and pay for her time to meet with me during the convention. Those four ladies who sat beside her at the airport all got a free pass from her to the backstage. I wish I had known who she was at the airport.

HM Dr. Uba Iwunwa

HM Dr. Uba Iwunwa showcases cultural diversity and lives by her quote *'My culture is my pride and identity.'* The proud Nigerian-Canadian Artist, Actress and #1: International Bestselling Guinness World Record author, Dr. Uba is a nine-time Honorary Doctorate Award recipient in Diplomacy, Philosophy, Peace and Human Rights, accredited with global Humanitarian Leadership. She is the World Peace Diplomatic Ambassador of Canada.

Dr. Uba grounds her work on the truth that music is the universal language for love that speaks to the soul. She understands the impact of culture and the way culture weaves itself into the collective consciousness and fabric of every Nation.

Dr. Uba believes that the exchange of culture through music, writing and performing arts opens the gateway to a deep understanding of each other's soul which yields respect for human dignity, a person's right to individuality, collective respect for humanity and human rights for all especially, this generation youth inheriting the world in front of them.

Dr. Uba's award-winning body of global humanitarian work, pride in cultural heritage exchange through her music, movies, educational lectures and performing arts, as well as her Human Rights advocacy and numerous various community charity work have earned her the face and voice for global peace and the Lifetime 'Queen of Peace' title. She is an alumnus of the United Nations University – AUGP/UNUGP USA.

Email: ojorima@gmail.com

www.ubaiwunwa.com

https://www.monarchyofyaya.com

#1 International Bestselling author

EVERY STORY STARTS SOMEWHERE

Pat Gennaro

My husband and I had a cafeteria a couple of years back and needed to hire someone to help out. When a young woman applied for the position of counter help, she was very quiet, meek and mild. She said she had worked in a restaurant before and asked if she could be paid in cash. My husband tried to find out why, but she did not say anything. My husband said he would do it for a short while, but eventually, we would have to pay her and take all the government taxes off. She nodded her head. We decided to hire this young woman. Her English was very proper English as she was from a country in Africa, and sometimes that would cause communication problems when giving directions as she did not always understand. As she started working for us we noticed that there would be times that our instructions or directions would be misinterpreted or not done the way we had explained to her.

One day one of our customers had come in for breakfast and asked our employee to make his eggs "over easy." When this customer got his eggs, they were hard and not over easy. The customer looked at my husband and laughed and said, "Is this the new way to do "over easy." My husband looked at the young lady and realized that our new employee may not have ever worked in a restaurant before. My husband came home that night and told me the breakfast story and his concerns about this lady's lack of kitchen experience. As the two of us discussed the situation, many thoughts went through our heads. As time went on, it had been obvious that she had not told us the truth, but we felt there had to be more to her story. We wondered if she was hiding from someone or here illegally.

My husband asked me to come in to work and try to get to know the new employee as she was so quiet that it was difficult to have a conversation with her. He felt that maybe having another female around would help her relax and open up. My presence did not really change anything, but we realized that even though she was quiet and shy, she was also very guarded. We had many discussions at the dinner table as to why she was very guarded and what she was hiding from us. The problem was she was a very likable, hard-working person. This was not the norm for my husband and me to hire someone with so much uncertainty and holes in their resume, but we felt she needed help. As time went on, her cooking skills improved, and her understanding of the kitchen and cooking lingo got better.

Then one day she came and asked my husband for two weeks' holiday. At this point, she had only been working for us for about one month. My husband was very baffled and not sure what to say to her. He tried to ask her some questions as to why she needed this time off so soon after starting this job. She was very vague and just said she needed to meet up with her cousin in the States. She also could not give us an exact date for this time off that she needed. She just kept saying around the end of October. After Thanksgiving weekend, we finally told her she needed to give exact dates so we could find someone to replace her for two weeks. She eventually gave us a date. We had told her she could have the time off if we could find a replacement to cover her. Luckily, we were able to. On the last Friday of October, we wished her a good holiday and hoped she enjoyed herself.

That same Friday night, my husband left for a fishing weekend. When he is on one of those fishing weekends, it was normal for us not to communicate till he was ready to come home or to let me know the approximate time he would be getting home. Saturday was a cold rainy day, and my daughter and I were just hanging out at home. In the late afternoon, the phone rang. As I went to pick it up, I saw a name, but it did not register who it belonged to. My daughter had answered at the same time. When I finally said, "Hello," I caught a piece of the conversation and then the phone line went dead.

I asked my daughter who it was. She said it was the lady from work and that she could not go on her holiday, and she needed to come to work on Monday. I phoned the number back that had registered on my phone, and it was our employee that answered. She was very distraught, upset, and tired. After a few minutes, I was able to understand that she missed her flight because she had been detained by immigration for five hours. By the time they let her go, she had missed her flight. She could not afford to buy another ticket, so she would not be going to meet her cousin and needed to come back to work on Monday.

I informed her I would need to speak to my husband as he had hired someone to cover her time away, but that would probably not happen till Sunday night as he was away. She became even more upset and stated she did not have any money left and needed this job. I said I would get back to her as soon as I could. I did reach out to my husband, and on Saturday night, he returned my call. I explained what had happened and what the situation was for our employee. He was upset because the person that was going to work for us for two weeks had rearranged her schedule so she could do us a favour and work for us. After some discussion, I phoned our employee back and told her to come into work on Monday morning.

So throughout her employment, we thought she did not have any money, housing or family. Well, shortly after this incident with her holiday mishap she finally gave us the full story.

In one way, we were right; she had no money other than what she earned from us. She rented a room from an older lady, and the only so-called family she had was a lady from her church that she called "her sister."

But she did have money in the States; she had a job, a car and a place to live. She also had a husband. Our employee had come up to Canada from the United States to visit her "sister," but it was at the time the Trump Administration had banned certain countries from entering the U.S.A. As it turned out, she was from one of those countries and could not go back to the States. She was stranded up here, she went to Canadian Immigration, and they started the process for her to become a refugee. By the time she came to work for us, she had been in Canada for two months. She had asked us to give her cash as pay as she had not gotten a Social Insurance Number yet and was terrified to tell anyone what was going on and really did not have any support other than her Case Worker.

When we asked her about going back to see her cousin, she finally opened up and told us she was really trying to go back to see her husband.

Meanwhile, her husband would not take her calls and had heard from this "sister" that his wife was working up here and making a life for herself here without him. He also did not believe that immigration detained her and would not let her go into the States. Her husband did eventually move here to Canada.

Our employee was a kind, generous, hard-working woman, but somehow, no fault of her own got caught in a mess she did not have any control over. She worked for us for over a year. During that time, she would send money home to her mother every two weeks. The day after receiving her paycheque, she would buy herself a new pair of shoes, boots or clothing trying to replace what she had left behind in the States. We were sad to see her go as she was an amazing employee (once she learned the kitchen lingo). But we were happy to see her fulfill her dream of going back to school to become a caseworker that worked with refugees.

From the beginning of our journey with this woman, we tried hard not to judge and assume she was down on her luck, but it took the journey to find out she was just caught in a rough spot but was working her way out of it.

Pat Gennaro

For most of my teenage years, I was raised just north of the city, (Toronto, Canada) but my parents encouraged my brother and me to explore the city. I moved to Toronto to attend college. Once I finished college and got my first job here, I never left. I met my husband here also. He was born and raised in Toronto. Neither of us wanted to move out of the city. I enjoy the quietness of living in the suburbs, but in 20 minutes, I know I can be downtown enjoying the city life. We have raised our three children here and taught them to navigate the city as well. We all enjoy watching sports and taking advantage of catching a pro baseball or hockey game, never mind all the concerts and various live theatres we can go to. As our children grow up to become adults, one has bought his own house with his fiancé, a second is back at University in her little apartment, and the youngest is still at home. I took an early retirement a couple of years ago from a very active career in nursing. I have just recently started a part-time job, something to keep me active. The company has only been in Canada for one year, and I am having lots of fun selling Magnetic Eyelashes. I can do most of it on the internet, but I still can interact with my clients by hosting a party or the client hosting her own party. I am looking forward to where this journey will take me.

Facebook: Pat Paul Gennaro
Instagram: @gennaropat
TikTok: @patgennaro
Website
www.toribellecosmetics.com/?webalias=lashesbypatsyg

HOW A BEACH BUM GOT ME TO RESET ON VALUES

Farahana Jobanputra

One of the greatest coaches I've ever met looks like a beach bum ... and in conversations with him, I'm now convinced that he is winning at life and living. Although we only chatted for a couple of days, the lessons I learned have stuck with me.

When I was growing up, it was always obvious to me that I stood out because I looked different from my peers. As a short, overweight, bespeckled, awkward teen, people saw me and always made instant judgements about me. My glasses were thick, like coca-cola bottles, weighing so much the pressure actually eroded the cartilage on my nose. I was painfully shy and introverted, seeking the safety of books rather than relationships, and while my classmates grew taller and benefitted from the change puberty brings, I remained the same.

To safely navigate social situations, I started to see how my appearance was off-putting, especially when compared to my peers. In order to improve myself, I began reading all kinds of self-help books, eventually finding Austin Kleon's famous saying, "You have to dress for the job you want, not the job you have ..." I had internalized this to mean that:

in my professional life, I had to dress like an executive in order to be seen as worthy of more responsibility to be 'taken seriously, I had to dress 'older,' or more 'professionally' – Ru

Paul is often quoted as saying, *"If you want to be taken seriously, wear a suit,"* and as he elaborates, you can't help but nod in agreement.

- to be more attractive, I had to wear clothes that were fashionable or on-trend, rather than wear clothes that I found comfortable, fun, or somehow reflective of my personality

- to 'fit in' with my peer group, I was frantic to look like the other girls in my class or to mimic the women I saw in fashion magazines or on TV

At the time when I met my coach, I was feeling exceptionally vulnerable. I was in my late teens, on this journey of self-discovery, sitting at a beach café in an oversize, long t-shirt (featuring a quirky anime character), which covered my bathing suit. My hair was loose, and I was deeply engrossed in my book. This was all uncharacteristic of me, as I almost always was dressed very conservatively and as neutral as possible to blend into the background; however, I was on vacation in a city I had never been in before and was free to be as quirky as possible.

I found myself to be jarringly brought back to reality with a booming "HEY! I LIKE YOUR SHIRT" followed by a laugh so heartfelt, you couldn't help but join in.

For all intents and purposes, one would never look at my coach and think that he's a 'great man' or that he would have insights on any aspect of life. Visually, he doesn't dress particularly well – his wardrobe would generously be described as 'lived in' or 'well loved.' His daily outfit rarely includes shoes or extends beyond flip-flops, as he lives on a beach. Clothes for him are functional and purposeful, fitting in with his lifestyle of doing yoga, surfing, catching up with people, thinking about life, or seeking out an interesting veggie bowl at a local café.

Had I met him in any other situation, I would have paid him no mind and probably tried to avoid actual contact with him, which is tragic because my life is so much richer for knowing him. Had it been any other situation, I would have probably dismissed him, but he was just so happy and full of life that I couldn't help myself but to seek him out for the short time I was holidaying in the area.

Talking to my coach, I started with the usual superficial small talk people start with, only to be quickly cut off (with another heartfelt laugh) as my coach quickly changed the conversation to thoughts on life, what I was going to do next (I was torn between different degree programs), and what my aspirations were. Today, as I reflect on these conversations, I realize that what my coach was really teaching me was to:

- Question my biases, and challenge what was causing me to form these judgements

- Question my reaction to people or situations, particularly when they didn't conform to my image of 'normal'

- Be open and willing to learn, check my assumptions, and expand my understanding

- Question my biases

Having grown up in a relatively sheltered family, I was also a scholarship student at a very elite private school. As a result, many of the people I knew were similar in appearance, background, and socioeconomic status. My peers had conditioned me to believe that who 'they' represented was the majority, and therefore, I had to change who I was by conforming to their standard to fit in.

My coach turned this upside down. Although he may have presented as a beach bum, he lived in a very exclusive area, in a home that cost millions to purchase. He had been exceptionally successful in work, and this allowed him to disengage with societal standards and instead focus on what interested him – talking to people, learning from them, investing in special businesses. I learned that he didn't have much regard for fashion because it didn't serve any purpose, and ensuring he was fully groomed wasn't high on his priority list.

Talking to him, I learned that the ideas I had formed about what it looked like to be successful, which was to have ostentatious wealth was largely created by companies and media. This was self-serving, as targeting young adults with newly printed credit cards (to be paid for by their parents) and high amounts of disposable income were largely part of a media ploy to build their consumer base. Taking this further, I learned that this came out of advertising campaigns in the 1960s to 1980s, as the advertising companies knew that building a younger consumer base was more likely to result in stronger brand loyalty and increased spending, coupled with a consumer who had a longer lifespan to make purchasing decisions over.

I also examined why I felt I had to conform to an image. Realizing that the only person imposing these limitations on me was myself was enormously freeing. Instead of studying magazines for the latest trends, I started to seek out ways to demonstrate my individuality, quirky nature, and personality in ways that were appropriate for the situation. In cases where I didn't care, I wore what I enjoyed, in many cases abandoning oversize, bulky clothes and neutral colours in favour of vibrant colours and sometimes outlandish costumes.

Questioning my reaction to people or situations, particularly when they didn't conform to my image of 'normal.'

Growing up, I was so afraid of being further identified as an outsider that I started to develop an instinctive reaction to anyone who also stood out. Being far from my environment allowed me to be more open-minded and relaxed. Building a friendship with someone so unaffected and uncaring of external experiences made it safe for me to go deeper and look beyond the external to what was more meaningful. It also made me rethink my assumptions of what was 'normal,' what was 'appropriate,' and why being confronted with an image outside of my limited experience was triggering. I also started on a journey of self-acceptance since it was obvious that although I would never look like others in my class, that had no bearing on any of my other skills or abilities.

The ability to travel was hugely eye-opening for me in this respect. I've been fortunate enough to live across four different continents, and seeing how others live and work taught me that there is no such thing as 'normal.' I also reset what my expectations of 'appropriate' are – I now focus more on behaviours than outward appearances. Having volunteered and worked in villages and remote areas, I often ran into people whose appearance didn't quite match mine.

In cases where I found this triggering, I also worked to understand what about the situation made me uncomfortable.

Be open and willing to learn, check my assumptions, and expand my understanding

Having travelled extensively and been fortunate enough to live in different areas with other international students, I learned that it was inappropriate to make widespread generalizations. For instance, I grew up with one version of "Indian curry"; however, travelling through different regions of India and Nepal, I learned that although the curry may have the same components (lentils, spices, rice), the mix was very distinctive to the region and there's no one homogenous definition for a dish, just like there isn't for people from a certain region, faith, education, or background.

Where I was once fearful of engaging with new people, I learned to be open to interacting with the world. My coach's booming and heartfelt laugh made me instantly warm to him and trust him, and from that, I've learned to use humour as a basis to form genuine interest in learning from others. I've also recognized that some of the most interesting people I have met are also introverts. As a result, I tend to now seek out other wallflowers and find that I have better quality conversations, build better relationships and have more memorable events.

Chance encounters can be beneficial because they nudge us to reframe our thinking. In my case, being challenged with someone who was so wildly different than my norm and being so quickly disarmed by genuine and heartfelt conversation led me on a fantastic journey of self-discovery. This, in turn, opened my horizons to explore other countries, environments, situations, all of which have made my life so much richer. I remain ever grateful to this chance encounter and for the benefit of meeting a coach who is now a dear friend.

Farahana Jobanputra

Farahana is a business transformation specialist and has launched projects over $1 billion in spend. With over 15 years of experience, working primarily within the Financial Services sector, Farahana is a proven leader, adept at building relationships and managing multi-disciplinary, global delivery teams. Farahana applies her specializations in law, cyber governance, project and change management to help client institutions be more agile, adopt digital practices, and comply with changing regulations using strong governance and risk mitigation practices.

In her spare time, Farahana is a diversity champion as a board member of a non-profit which encourages underprivileged and under-represented youths to explore STEEM careers. She holds a Master of Laws from The University of Toronto specializing in Technology Innovation (digital assets, Blockchain, cyber security, privacy), an MBA from Brandeis University, and certifications in Project and Change Management, and in Cyber Security, Forensics and Governance.

THINK BEFORE YOU JUDGE

Daphne Soares

Many times I get asked, "Where are you from?" I ask myself, "Why am I asked this question all the time?" I find that if I do respond, I get the answer, "You don't look or sound like it." Seriously??? People are so judgmental. How can they know me inside and out? Some do it to feel superior and better about themselves, while others mostly form their opinions from the exterior rather than the interior. To know the interior, we need to have spent quality time with that person. You cannot know a person fully overnight. We all are much more than what meets the eye.

Now, what can all of us do about these kinds of people? Can we make them think differently? Maybe yes and maybe no. There are two sides to a coin. This makes me look at what's within my control that can help change the situation, firstly for myself and then for the other person. I have come to realize that if I keep an open mind and have a positive mind, I can give the other person a fair chance to make the transition and change their approach without getting myself upset or frustrated. This helps me personally to be happier and a more approachable person, enabling me to look within before I look beyond.

Judging is something we all do all the time, and it can be damaging when it comes to people. We need to make the change we want to see in the other and put ourselves in the other person's shoes. We should not judge unless we are ready to be judged. This makes things less complicated and better. Let us look at some common issues. Imagine a divorced girl.

Society begins to label her as one with a bad character. Is it so? Well, it takes two hands to clap, and we do not know the exact situation that caused it. In other cases, when we see a child misbehaving, we accuse the mother of not doing her duty and raising the kid wrongly. While when we see a fat boy in a restaurant, we say, "He should eat less and lose weight." We see someone panhandling on the road, and we say, "He should get a job." Do we even know what their story is or what they have gone through? Most of the time, we don't. Before finding fault with others and passing judgement, we need to pause and take a good look deep within ourselves and be the best version of ourselves that we can.

The idea of "us" and "them" is so outdated and puts blocks in our pathway. It builds walls between people. Judgement is what divides us from others, be it clothes, the home one comes from, where they live, finances and most commonly, one's colour. Why are these things affecting you? Are you going to fill the gaps in their needs and wants? Are they asking you to maintain them? Why does it matter so much to you? All this does not bring us closer; rather, it is the ruin of many friendships, families and relationships in the workplace. If we look skin-deep, we all have the same flesh and blood no matter where we are or come from. So why discriminate and look down on any human being? The person you look down on in shabby clothes might be a very important person or someone who can teach you the most, someone you might need one day in a given situation. Closing our minds leaves no room for learning, bonding and broadening our horizons. Why do we need to put limitations on our own growth and learning?. You need to stay open-minded and positive. You need to change your perspective by looking for the good in others. Here are few easy steps that will help you to avoid being judgmental:

Positive thinking: think positively and try to see the positive side in the other person.

Separate actions from personality: sometimes circumstances and situations can cause a person to act a certain way, e.g. the person in your office declines participating in the company pool. It could be that he has huge bills to pay or has a sick member in the family and needs to save every penny.

Observe when you judge: try to nip that thought and feed your mind with something positive, *e.g.*, the height of the person, their smile, a kind word or deed.

Put yourself in that person's shoes; how would you like others to treat you in a given situation? Why is that person stingy? Has he faced a major financial loss? Or the person that is very reserved; has he always been suppressed and never allowed to voice his or her thoughts?

Look for commonalities: a way that you can connect with the person, e.g. a book, an event or experience. Have a dialogue and avoid a monologue. Everyone wants to be heard.

Count your blessings: see the good you have in your life and be thankful for it. Do not look down on another who doesn't have material wealth, and most of all, do not show off about anything. Remember, pride comes before a fall.

Be compassionate: it is the opposite of being judgmental. Do your best to empathize with others, be ready to hear and feel them. Come with a heart to serve and not to be served.

Keep reminding yourself that what you give comes back to you a hundredfold in many ways.

Expectation: this is a major area that leads to numerous issues in any relationship. Be it at home, friends, community or in the workplace. We always expect certain behaviour and responses from others. When we do not get what we expect, friction starts. Why not voice it out in a mature way? Tell the person why you expected a certain response or behaviour, e.g. on your birthday, you expected your friend to wish you a happy birthday first thing in the morning, and that person woke up late and rushed to work. This was not intentional. Your friend had no intention to miss it, and there you sit, all upset and start avoiding the person completely. I know it sucks when your friend does this, but if you do not make the effort to try and find out what caused it before you pass judgement, you are the one that suffers.

Use every experience: use it as a means for your own growth and to learn something new from everyone regardless of their caste, colour, race, creed, nationality or colour. A person who has the talent you do not possess might be able to teach you a new skill or language.

Socialize and travel: the more you interact with different kinds of people, the more you will become welcoming and broad-minded. You will begin to see that not everything and everyone is the way you perceive them to be. Be a lifelong learner. Share your thoughts and ideas and let others do the same.

Read books, magazines and surf the internet: learning never stops. There is a lot to be found in books, magazines and on the internet if we pick the right stories that can enlighten our mind and thinking. Invest in yourself and use your time wisely.

Step out of your comfort zone: explore new opportunities, try different cuisines, modes of transport, interact with different cultures and experience life yourself. Stop sitting on the fence and passing judgement. It will get you nowhere.

Overcome limiting beliefs: have you got a belief that a person of a certain colour, nationality or dress is inferior or superior to you? Why? Personally interact with people with an open mind. Do not pass a judgment just because others said so. Do not judge a book by its cover but dive deep and explore the situation for yourself.

Examine your judgmental attitude: why are you judging a particular person or situation that way? Take time to answer before you react.

As human beings, we all want to be loved, welcomed, heard, understood and given a fair chance. We want others to respect and value us. So let us do away with judgment and replace it with love and empathy. Only then can we grow. Are you ready to leave a legacy and make those choices in life that can change the world around you? Don't wait for tomorrow. Do it today and let it begin with you.

Daphne Soares

Daphne Soares is the Founder and CEO of Carousel Moms Business and Leadership Coaching.

She is the first Pakistani to be ranked among the Top 10 Female Coaches in 2021 by Yahoo Finance and is also a Guinness World Records, International Bestselling author of two books.

She is the Awardee of:

'Honorary Doctorate' from The Global University International in association with HRH Queen Nadia Harihir, HRH Queen Dr.Elizabeth Lucas II and Princess Amb. Dr.Catherine Comandante Sanghil

'The Most Inspirational Leader and International Hero Award' by The Global University International in association with HRH Queen Nadia Harihir, HRH Queen Dr.Elizabeth Lucas II and Princess Amb. Dr.Catherine Comandante Sanghil

She was also awarded:

Asia's Outstanding Woman Leadership and Mentoring Award

Shaurya Samman Award

Ramada 'Best Sales and Marketing Award'

Knowledge World Skills Development Trainers Award Pakistan.

15 Years Volunteer's Sodality 'Service Without Limits Award' from UAE.

Dr.Sarvepalli Radhakrishan 'Commendable Contributions Award.

Daphne is also a nominee for:

Asian International Excellence Award

Awarded Intellects International 'Woman of Vigor Award'

She is a mother, a Business and Leadership Coach, International Speaker and Mentor. She has gone from a career woman with a 9 to 5 job to a Homemaker, Masters' Catechist, Counsellor, Psychotherapist and Hypnotherapist.

Daphne is a certified Masters' Catechist with Distinction from Dayton University, Ohio, USA and UAE. A Post Diploma holder in NLP, Counselling, Hypnotherapy and Psychotherapy from Anugraha Institute of Counselling, Psychotherapy and Research, Meta Dynamics, Business and Leadership Coaching from Australia and UAE. A member of the ICG and ICF.

She takes pride in seeing the success of her clients and others. She is passionate in helping to empower women, especially moms, to find the right balance in their own carousels of life, create a thriving business without feeling overwhelmed, set SMART goals and build great rapport with their teams and clients for business success, live a happy and balanced life, overcome limiting beliefs and set healthy boundaries. She also works with companies to overcome disruptive leadership within the organization.

Daphne has been working as a certified Coaching Professional who specializes in helping people cope with their mindset, business and leadership issues. She coaches her clients in a way that utilizes both their heads and their hearts. She first learned about coaching when she hit a roadblock in her own life and was struggling to move past it. The techniques she developed were so successful that friends and family began asking me for help with their own challenges. This motivated her to turn her newfound passion into a full-time career.

Overall, Daphne is an amazingly versatile woman whose commendable work is an epitome for other women to look up to for inspiration and vast experience.

She empowers women through 1:1 personalized and Group Coaching.

Daphne believes: "*The Power is Within you! Break FREE from what is holding you back.*"

Daphne may be reached on the links below:

https://www.linkedin.com/in/daphne-soares-530685201

daphnesoares@carouselmoms.com

https://www.carouselmoms.com

She is also on Facebook and Instagram:

https://www.facebook.com/carouselmoms/

https://www.instagram.com/carouselmoms/

Don't Judge and Don't Be Judged

Pravin Patel (#DRPPP)

I understand the hurt that comes from being judged by your appearance. When it is something that you cannot change, and others judge you because of it — it feels so unfair. It is so hard to build your self-confidence when this happens to you as a child.

I used to be so thin during my childhood. I would exercise with my father, I also used to do yoga and meditation with him. My father used to call me "The Slim Bodybuilder" to inspire me to gain weight, but "The Slim Bodybuilder" tag used to hurt me a lot. To cover my thin arms, I used to wear long-sleeve shirts.

To cover my slim legs, I preferred to wear pants rather than shorts. I was very academic, and I preferred to be involved with books rather than to go out. I was also very shy. I visited my family doctor several times with my father to investigate how to gain weight. Nothing he recommended seemed to work. Yet, I was physically and mentally strong, and I trained.

I ran my first full marathon in October 2015. I was inspired by Terry Fox as well as Faujaji from India. This proved to me that I was a capable athlete, and so I kept going. Those that have run marathons will attest to the fact that it is not only the physical exertion that brings success, it is also the mental focus and determination not to give up.

I ran 16 full marathons by God's grace and your blessings. The first and second marathons were in one week. It takes a lot of physical stamina to endure the exhaustion that comes with a marathon. I also had to recover sufficiently to go ahead with the second marathon. The exhilaration of completing that second marathon encouraged me to keep going. The sixth and seventh marathons were in one week too. Also, the tenth and eleventh marathons were in one week. By this time, I began to gain not only self-confidence but an assurance that I had overcome the negative feelings of being judged for being slim.

The last four marathons were run in one month by God's grace and your blessings.

If DR.PPP becomes The Marathon Man, so can you.

I was born in a third-world, developing country, Mother India. I suffered from an inferiority complex because of my English during medical college. I failed so many times during medical college that I stopped counting. It took such a long time to publish my first book because I started to share with the world the details about my upcoming book. One day my father got angry at me on the phone and told me to stop writing because there was so much delay in finishing my first book. My father is not only my father but also my godfather, but this time I decided that either my book would be finished by the end of the day on May 1, 2017, or I would die by jumping into Niagara Falls. However, that never happened, and my first book launch was hosted by Raymond Aaron, my publisher and New York Times Bestseller.

Jack Canfield was the main guest at my launch by God's grace and your blessings. Jack Canfield is "*The Secret*" movie Celebrity and the co-creator of the series "*Chicken Soup for the Soul.*". He didn't let the 144 publishers, who rejected his first book, "*Chicken Soup For the Soul*" discourage him or stop him from getting it published. I didn't let my father stop me from writing my first book and getting it published either.

When I wrote the manuscripts for three books in 33 hours, my father congratulated me.

I wrote my first book, "*You are the Celebrity,*" in English, which became "*The Celebrity Guru*" Award Winner. I wrote the chapter in my second book, "*Magnetic Entrepreneur-A Personality That Attracts,*" in English, which became a #1 International Bestseller by God's grace and your blessings. It pushed Elon Musk's book to #2 and Steve Jobs's book to #5.

I wrote the chapter in my third book, "*Magnetic Entrepreneur Mastermind - Breaking Free,*" in English, which also became a Canadian Bestseller.I wrote the chapter in my fourth book, "*Magnetic Entrepreneur-Celebrities Keeping It Real*" in English, which also became a #1 International Bestseller.

I wrote my Bio in my fifth book, "*Magnetic Entrepreneur - World Renowned,*" in English, which became a Guinness World Records, #1 International Bestseller. I wrote my chapter in my sixth book, "*Magnetic Entrepreneur-Covid-19 The Lockdown,*" in English, and it too became a Canadian Bestseller.I wrote the chapter in my seventh book, "*Magnetic Entrepreneur- The Blessings Of Covid-19,*" in English, which also became an International Bestseller.

I wrote the chapter in my eighth book, "*Magnetic Entrepreneur- Finding My Why*" in English, which became International Bestseller too. I am the author of this chapter in this book, "*Don't Judge A Book By Its Cover – Poor Clothes Can Hide a Rich Heart,*" in English. I am a Guinness World Record author of my Bio in the upcoming book, "*Magnetic Entrepreneur - Go Getters Getting It Done*," in English. I am the author of a chapter in the upcoming book "*Magnetic Entrepreneur - The Spiritual CEO*" in English.

Thank you, Raymond Aaron, the publisher of my first book.Thank you, Robert J Moore, the publisher of all my other books.

My books changed my life. My books changed thousands of people's lives. I was the same person then. I am the same person now. I will be the same person in the future. The way people used to look at me before I became an author and after being an author changed. I get more respect, and I am known as an authority. My books brand me. Being an author made me so much more than all my degrees combined. I got offered interviews after I became an author. I interviewed people from all walks of life from all over the world.

If I can write, so can you.

If I can write books in English, so can you.

Believe in your wildest dreams.

Don't let anybody steal your dreams.

Just Do It Now.

If Trump can win, so can you.

You have the celebrity day.

You have the celebrity life.

You are the Celebrity.

You are the Magnetic Entrepreneur.

DON'T JUDGE. Don't allow anybody's judgment to steal your wildest dreams.

Don't Judge a book by its cover.

Don't Judge people by their race, religion, sex, colour, body size, location, health, wealth etc.

Don't Judge your family members, relatives, friends or strangers. Don't allow anybody, including your family members, relatives, friends or strangers, to judge you.

Live and let live.

Dr. Pravin Patel (#DRPPP)

The Celebrity Guru DR.PPP's full name is DR. Pravin, Prahladbhai Patel. He was born on Temple Street, Jhulasan, in the state of Gujarat, India, the home of the family of celebrity NASA astronaut, Sunita Williams, as well as a famous Muslim Goddess Dolo Ma Temple.

The Celebrity Guru, DR.PPP, has met thousands of celebrities from all over the world, e.g., Bollywood celebrities, Hollywood celebrities, spiritual celebrities, celebrity politicians, celebrity cricketers, celebrity tennis players, celebrity entrepreneurs, celebrity authors, and more. DR.PPP has collected their autographs, photographs, and interviewed them to share their secrets to success with you through his first book, *You Are The Celebrity*," which is about how to become famous. To get a free copy of the first chapter of the book, please visit: youarethecelebritybook.com

DR.PPP studied Medicine in India and homeopathy in Canada.

He served in the Canadian Army as an engineer to fulfill his childhood dream to become an engineer as well as to serve the nation.

For DR. PPP's rates and availability as The Celebrity Speaker as well as The Celebrity Coach, please visit:

youarethecelebritybook.com

Call: 416 543-5231

IT'S NOT YOUR FAULT

Karen Seegert

We all know that looks can be deceiving, things are not always what they seem and forming opinions based on appearances is wrong. But we do it anyway.

Our world is fast-paced; we make quick decisions and judgements about everything and everyone. We are taught this in our formative years through our cultural upbringing, trust of "authoritarians," educational systems and religious teachings. We are bombarded by media messages and addicted to technology that delivers these controlling directives. This indoctrination has infiltrated every aspect of our lives and influenced our thoughts and behaviours.

From an early age, we are told how we should look, talk and behave. We are taught that we are not good enough, that we are sinners and that if we follow along and do as we are told, then we will be vindicated or rewarded; life will be grand. We will be happy when we agree to live by these rules. We have been taught to show the world our worth by mirroring back what we think we should be or do, and this pathetic way of being has become instinctual.

Understand - this auto-response is not your fault – you have been programmed. We collectively inherited a generational DNA that prepares us to adapt to the ever-changing world, but it also generates habits sanctioned by external forces, telling us what is acceptable, how we should think and feel, with zero consideration for our true nature.

The reality is that when we become coherent with these low, negative frequencies, we can be easily influenced, and our common sense and logic are then replaced by fear and confusion. This is not my opinion but a reflection of the law of vibration. But, the reverse holds true too – it is not easy to assert control on an empowered person.

We make presumptions about others based on what we observe — their skin colour, their clothing, their apparent social status, the ethnic group we associate them with, their gender, the symbols of their religious beliefs they probably conform to and the overall appearance of their body. We form an opinion of the character, credibility and worthiness of a person from everything that we can "see" externally. This bias is so twisted!

I am sure you agree that every living being is different, so it is absolutely impossible to know how anyone truly thinks or feels. If we removed all their worldly possessions and outer influences, their divine spirit would be revealed with a unique story to share.

My entire life, I have struggled to fit in because I have always been an independent thinker. That mindset has led to a "whole lotta" life experiences, so diverse that I often joke that I could be the subject of a talk show for a month — just pick a topic! Some people listen with interest as I tell my tales, some gain a morsel of insight when they internalize my words, but others resort back to their fishbowl existence, surmising that I am spoiled, entitled or delusional.

I realize that what others think about me is none of my business, but it's sad that the collective perception is so shallow. I chose to embrace my deservedness, and my life is blessed because I listen to my spirit, and there is absolutely nothing stopping you from adopting this attitude.

In the midst of the world's chaos and seemingly hopeless despair, I made a conscious decision to be a catalyst for change, to introduce people to ideas, methods, technologies, products and therapies to create awareness in their lives and rekindle the connection to their inner world and their purpose in life. The only regulator of peace and true understanding lives within you. When you make a simple shift in consciousness and identify with how you feel and embody serenity and peace, you will transform your life.

The external world will not fulfill you anymore; you will have an aversion to the lower frequencies, the old stereotypical behaviours will no longer be satisfying – they will have lost their meaning, and you too will feel the unconditional love in your heart. This is defined by many as the process of 'waking up.'

If you are not convinced that your skewed opinions were intentionally implanted, then answer these questions: How much time do you devote to prejudging others? Do you truly believe that having a tally of "likes" on a social media posts really matters? Are you honestly so caught up in the hysteria that you don't bother to learn and understand how your amazing body and mind function? Have you willingly forfeited your innate intelligence? Why is it not obvious that the agenda is to intentionally create dissention and foster polarization? How did you allow yourself to be consumed by the purposeless hypocrisy? And the most important question of all - how do you really feel?

Imagine a world where each person embraced their true nature and value and shared their authentic self to contribute, rather than prejudging and determining a person's value based on a superficial glimpse. I understand if you are struggling with the notion that you alone can alter the predominate reign over your life, but indeed you can. I implore you to shift your way of thinking now!

"Time is of the essence" is not just another idiom. At our current stage of evolution, we rarely come across the truth and the things we need to be thinking about. We live our lives accepting as a society, that which we are told and the reports produced by a governing body that ultimately have nothing to do with the truth of our human nature. We are concerned with everything surrounding us in our life; the clothes we wear, the food we eat, the prestigious things we own, what we think others think about us and on and on. We actually think that we are being polite and reasonable.

Well - time is up, people. We can't continue to exist by blaming and criticizing without taking self-responsibility. We need to wake up to the fact that each and every person today affects the situation of the world through the choices they make. Choose wisely, and if you need help, seek a mentor to guide you towards enlightenment and reconnect with the power that lies within your beautiful soul. And if you don't know where to find that person, contact me.

Your life story, written by you, is unique and filled with lessons, tribulations and blessings. The cover is simply a protective jacket. You have to look inside to see the contents. Know that you can create a self-portrayal that is a true reflection of the magnificence within. When you raise your consciousness, you will empower others, and together we can evolve to a purposeful existence. The only thing that matters in life is the true spirit within each of us.

Karen Seegert

Karen Seegert is an Energy medicine educator, scar therapist, biofeedback technician, PEMF practitioner and Sanza specialist, founder of Cell Energy Therapy Inc, Cell Regeneration System Inc, and Innovation Therapy and Treatment Inc.

Karen is on a mission to create awareness around the amazing "Sanza" technology, which she explains is foundational in achieving an optimal state of well-being. "The number one thing you need to be healthy is energy." www.sanza.info

Feel free to contact her karen@cellenergytherapy.com

HOW TO LEARN TO JUDGE OTHERS ONLY WITH LOVE FROM THE HEART

Nadene Joy

Growing up, I recall for as far back as I can remember, as young as four years old, seeing business men and women dressed in nice suits, elegant dresses and attire and thinking they had it all together and must be "successful." They appeared to be "perfect" to others looking from the outside in on their life and also perhaps to the rest of the world. It wasn't until years later and after being immersed in the corporate and coaching worlds that I came to realize this was a false preconceived presumption I had made and we all make to some degree and fed into. At this time, this "observation," proved to be just an illusion and facade that was formulated deep in my subconscious mind based on the many subliminal and conscious messages observed and heard on TV, in media, movies, with family and friends and so forth. This form of societal conditioning begins the day we are born.

The Corporate Truth

As I grew older, graduated from high school and University, I landed my first job as an exploration geologist for a global oil company. It was here that I realized very quickly that many professionals dressed surprisingly very similarly. We've all heard the saying "dress for success." The way you dress is kind of an unspoken respect and "perfection" so to speak that was expected by many, especially the higher up the corporate ladder you climbed. The higher up position you held, the more it was observed that people, both men and women alike, wore professional attire. The higher up the corporate ladder you were, the more others looked at you as if you were "better than them" and on a non-spoken "pedestal of perfection." Most people look at those in higher authority and position and who are well dressed, me included for many years, and automatically think also that they are or must be smarter, better off financially, have the "perfect" family and life and so forth. We place them above us and forget that they are, in fact, human too and that no one is perfect.

The Comparison Cycle and Trap

We must remove the invisible masks once and for all. We must take a closer look at how we judge others who appear to have it all together externally and place them on a pedestal based on their success, financial wealth, their beauty and strikingly handsome looks, their level of faith, or simply on shear intelligence alone. Professionals in these roles must learn to be more real, vulnerable and authentic and take the mask of perfection and the status quo off once and for all. It is human nature to default to a "less than" facade or perhaps of feeling of "I am not good enough." Unless we become consciously aware of our comparison and judgemental thoughts of ourselves and others, it becomes all too easy to get caught up in this unending comparison and self-destructive cycle of degrading and sabotaging ourselves and others. One of the fastest ways to feel like a victim and degrade your self-worth and confidence is to compare yourself to others.

Breaking Free from Comparison

Did you know that many people who are the most seemingly confident, also compare themselves to others? When we show up from a egotistical point of view versus from an authentic heart-centred perspective, we exude a sense of pride and pride itself is not authentic confidence. Even if we never speak or think critical and comparitive thoughts, the odds are that if we "secretly and silently" put others down. It is a destructive rescuing strategy to ease our own internal pain that has possibly been repressed around not being good enough or lacking self-worth internally. When you live a life of comparison it is unhealthy and toxic as you can go from putting yourself down one moment to criticizing others in the next, which is an excruciatingly exhausting way to live. It takes a lot of energy to keep this comparison cycle going, especially when there is nothing good that comes from it.

As a top leader today, and a professional who previously placed others on pedestals and judged others subconsciously on a regular basis, I have much to say about this topic from my own personal experience. As a top coach, I have worked personally with thousands of people all around the world, from the homeless to some of the top 1% of millionaires and billionaires of our time. The thing I have learned is that you never know what someone else is going through, suffering from, or has gone through based on their outward appearance or image alone. Some of the most outwardly appearing professionals and even everyday joyful citizens are suffering silently the most. I also know and have met some of the wealthiest leaders who wear blue jeans and T-shirts vs the traditional suit or business attire. These examples alone go to show the sheer importance of not "judging someone by their cover." As I always say, you never know who is sitting next to you on a plane, in a coffee shop or beside you at a conference or place of worship. For example, on many occasions in my own life, this has occurred. A few examples I will share were when I flying and ended up sitting directly beside very prolific individuals who looked like simple ordinary citizens. One was the father of one of the most famous movie animators at Pixar of all time, and the other was one of the most popular award-winning musicians and his manager in Canada at the time! These are just a few of many examples in my life of times where who I thought was just an ordinary person turned out to be someone extraordinary which was completely unexpected. When we judge others, it somehow makes us feel less than ourselves. I always say to be open and receptive to "expect the unexpected in life free from all judgements and expectations!"

This comparison phenomenon and cycle is more common than you might think. A survey conducted by Psychology Today found that 23.4 percent of people said that they misjudged someone based on their appearance two or three times per month; 9.4 percent said once a month; 17.4 percent said two or three times per week; and 4.7 percent said they misjudged someone, simply based on their appearance, every day. Implicit biases are pervasive.

"In order to be a more objective leader, we must first understand that we are all inherently subjective, and we all have unconscious biases of some degree. Studies reveal that most of us had definite entrenched stereotypes by the time we were five years old." As children, we constantly appraised our environment and formed conclusions about our world. For example, if we didn't observe faces of colour in our Saturday morning cartoons, we may have assumed that it was possibly not as good. Perhaps if we didn't see women holding leadership positions of influence and power, we may have interpreted that to mean women were somehow "less than" men. If we, as men, grew up never seeing the male role models in our lives cry and honour their emotions, perhaps we may have assumed if we show emotions as an adult, we are considered weak or lesser in society. These are only a few examples of many where we try to make sense of our world through perceptions only and not our own truths.

One of the main reasons we judge people is the lack of information. I'd like to pause for a moment and ask you a question. Are you certain that you know all the facts about the person you are judging or placing on a pedestal? Most of the time, we may have judged a situation without knowing the whole story. It is very important to hold off on any judgements until we know all facts. It's one of the clearest reasons why we shouldn't judge other people at all and simply just treat others as we wish to be treated in the first place.

You define yourself and Have Greatness Inside of You waiting to be Unleashed

Exercise: Next time you are triggered in any way by someone else's success, appearance or financial abundance, I'd like you to stop and pause for a few moments to write down all the qualities you admire most about that person. Once your list is complete, I want you to realize you have all of these qualities inside of you that are currently lying dormant and have not been brought to the surface to be permanently unleashed. All the greatness you need lies within you; sometimes it just takes someone else to be your mirror to finally see it for yourself and to really feel and know your worth once and for all in the deepest parts of your being. Earl Nightingale has so eloquently summed this up: "When you judge others, you do not define them, you define yourself."

One of the greatest lessons I have learned in life is that we have no place to judge the lives of others based on their outward appearance and expression as it is only each individual person who knows their own pain, circumstances and renunciation they have gone through. Judge less, accept more, criticize less, love more, and you will restore your happiness. Happiness is an inside job. No one can make you happy as it is a choice you make each and every day to make the world a better place. It all starts with believing in yourself first!

The power of belief and faith is limitless.

Did you know that if you wrote a lie on a card and read it often enough, you would start to believe it?

"Believe, and your belief will actually create the fact." - William James

Listen and Act with Love from The Heart

The moral here is to be compassionate and not judge the worth or value of someone or something by outward appearance alone. Take note that appearances are often misleading, anything that is essential is invisible to the eyes, things aren't always as they seem, looks can be deceiving and lastly — and most importantly — that one sees clearly only with the heart for it recognizes the truth of the soul. It is essentially who we are on the inside and random acts of loving-kindness that shines outward to the world that makes us most attractive of all. That being said, physical appearance still matters in our ever-evolving world. It's just the stereotypes and judgements that desperately need to be laid to rest. In fact, psychology research has actually found that dressing more formally actually makes people think differently. When people dress up they feel more powerful, and this allows them to make better decisions and actually perform as a "more competent person in that role." Dress professionally, but don't forget to be a good person at the same time and always treat others equally as best you can. First impressions do count. According to Forbes Magazine, within the first seven seconds of meeting, people will have a solid impression of who you are — and some research suggests a tenth of a second is all it takes to start determining traits like trustworthiness.

In closing, I would like to provide a few ways we can practice being non-judgemental towards ourselves and others:

- Practice curiosity and ask questions, practice empathy and compassion, positively reframe the situation, don't pass judgements, avoid stereotyping, notice your thoughts (and let negative thoughts go), take time to better understand the person, be accepting, look for the goodness in all people, bring greater joy and unconditional love back into your life and lastly, remember, it is those who behave the most unlovingly that need love the most!

As John 7:24 states: *"Do not judge by appearances, but judge with right judgment."* Be a person of integrity and character, above all. Being able to recognize your judgmental thoughts enables you to reframe them and view them differently. It is here where greater positive transformation transpires and takes root to make the world a better place for all of humanity.

It all starts with YOU!

Nadene Joy

Nadene Joy is a top advisor, executive leadership strategist and global mindset coach who helps top leaders get unstuck, achieve their goals, live balanced lives personally and professionally and achieve their wildest dreams. She is an Executive Coach and Trainer, Certified CMHA Psychological Health and Safety Advisor, NLP Practitioner, avid mental health advocate, ambassador of suicide awareness, alleviating hunger and combatting homelessness in communities worldwide, Speaker, international bestselling author and former top oil executive and petroleum exploration Geologist. Nadene is also a director and advisor on various prestigious and non-boards, both locally and internationally. She also has been awarded several achievements of excellence throughout her career, including the 2021 International Women of Substance Award by The St. Mother Theresa University (India) and TISGS Award of Business Excellence In Social Impact under the Patronage of H.E. Sheikh Eng. Salem Bin Sultan Al Qasimi (Dubai).

Nadene Joy is the CEO of Nadene Joy Consulting Inc., an accredited A+ BBB member and is Chair/Founder of The Lead 2 Impact Summit. She has been featured in top media outlets, including USA TODAY, CBC, ihearrtadio in NYC, Fox, The Globe and Mail, and NBC, and is the author of "Uncover Your Purpose: Heal and Share Your Gifts With the World" and "Love is...A Guide to the Power of Love." She is also the co-author of "Cracking The Rich Code Vol. 4" with Kevin Harrington, hit star of the TV Show, SharkTank and business icon Jim Britt.

Nadene Joy is truly passionate about being an impactful leader, mother to four beautiful children and friend who makes a positive difference in our world through taking bold action in sharing her authentic wisdom, experiences, God-given gifts, serving others with loving-kindness and bringing hope, love, joy, purpose, healing, inspiration and love, to all she encounters.

Nadene@NadeneJoy.com
www.NadeneJoy.com
http://linkedin.com/in/nadenejoy

May I Have Your Attention, Please?

Olivia Lombardo

I know that a lot of people get judged for the littlest things. Their skin colour, religion, the history of their country - anything! People just look at a person that doesn't look the same as them, and they're convinced that the person did something bad. I've had my fair share of people judging me, and let me tell you; it does not feel good. Actually, speaking of judging people, here is a little story that I have.

One time I was with one of my friends at the park, and then a boy in our grade noticed us, and he started talking to us. It was pretty normal until the boy made a really racist joke. You see, my mom's Korean and my dad's Italian. But I look more like my mom than my dad, meaning I look more Korean than Italian. Do you want to know what the boy said? He said, "All Asians look like this." And he squinted his eyes. My friend and I just looked at each other. "That's racist." We said at the same time. It turned out that the boy didn't even know what "racist" meant. And the joke? He got it from his uncle.

And you think that was bad? Listen to this:

I used to go to dance lessons when I was around 8 or 9. At the lessons, there was this girl who wasn't the nicest. She was pretty rude to most people, especially me. It didn't really bother me that much until the pandemic.

So, it was about early January last year when she said something really bad. Everyone already knew about the coronavirus and the "eating bat" situation in China. So when the instructor was handing out the dance costumes, everyone was gathered around in a circle talking about random things. Again, this was pretty normal. But then someone asked what our backgrounds were. I didn't really think much of it, and I said I was half Korean, half Italian. But then the rude girl looked at me with a mean look on her face, and she said, "My mom says that all Asian people are dirty."

Do you know what that tells me? We, kids, often repeat what we hear from our parents or relatives. Sometimes, we don't even know what it means. We just hear someone say it and repeat it, and we think it's "cool" because it came from a grown-up. Most of our morals and beliefs we get taught at home. Parents are our best teachers, and most of us are very likely to become like them when we grow up. Our parents probably learned from their parents. It only takes one person to start a chain of people judging others. If we keep looking at others with judgemental eyes, our society will become less tolerant and unforgiving. I mean - fast forward to 40 years from now. People would judge someone even if they had one less eyelash than them! If you want to change this from happening, it's really simple! Have an open mind and acknowledge there are many people different than you. That's it. But I know that there are going to be people who don't change even if the whole world was telling them to. And I have one thing to say to those people: It sucks to be them.

There's actually another thing that I haven't talked about. Muslims.

You know, people are so terrible to them for no reason. They think that all Muslims are "bad people." This makes my blood boil. Let me clear this up for you, buddy; not all Muslims are bad. Yes, there are a few of them who are bad people. But that's literally just like every race on this planet. There are a few white people who are bad. There are a few black people who are bad. There are a few Hispanic people who are bad. But that's normal. In fact, that's so normal that I don't even know how people don't know that.

Actually, I was talking to my mom the other day, and it turned out that she didn't know what a niqab was! (A niqab is a veil that covers your whole face except your eyes.). I ended up telling her, but that's okay because she was willing to learn. Honestly, if everyone was like that, then our society wouldn't be as judgemental as it is right now.

There's actually this lady who I follow on social media. She makes awesome videos about how she converted into being a Muslim. And you know why I follow her? It's because she knows that she's going to get hate mail for it. She knows that some people are not going to like her. But she did it anyway. If it makes her happy, then why should she care about other people's stupid opinions?

Ah, opinions. So dumb but so smart at the same time. Don't get me wrong - everybody is entitled to have their own opinion, but sometimes, people really need to shut up about them. Take the Covid pandemic as an example. Some people think masks keep you safe, while others think that masks are stupid and that they don't help with the situation. Even with the vaccine! Some people think that the vaccine is legitimate, and that it works, but then there are a handful of people who think that the vaccine is a load of nonsense. I even have some close relatives who aren't willing to get the vaccine. Sure, it's pretty annoying, but what can you do?

Opinions can lead to terrible things sometimes. In fact, most wars are started based on opinions. But the thing is, opinions are really hard to change. Think about the people who think the Earth is flat! There's so much evidence proving the Earth is round, but they just brush it off and say that it's "fake." See what I mean? It's super hard to change someone's opinion. I mean - the only way to change a flat-earther's opinion is to take them on a spaceship so they can see that the Earth is round, which will never happen.

My point is: opinions almost never change. But the best thing to do about that is to just leave it alone. Sure, it could be wrong or bad, but starting a fight over it is even worse.

Here's another thing that I find really ignorant. It's when people dumb things down for someone with a disability. For example, some people might talk slower when they're speaking to someone who's deaf. Or, someone might make work easier for someone who's autistic. Some people think that if someone has a disability, they're automatically less capable than someone who doesn't. But you never know, that disabled person could become more successful than you'll ever be!

I'm almost 100% sure that everyone has judged someone in the past. You, me, everyone! But as humans, it's our nature to judge. All I'm saying is that we should keep the judging to a minimum. And I know that some people reading this will completely ignore what I'm saying. Like I said, you can't change opinions just like that. People have to learn by themselves, or with a little help. Just don't force your beliefs on someone else. It's not the end of the world if you have a different opinion than someone else. It's not like you have to agree with them or something. Just carry on with your day!

Olivia Lombardo

My name is Olivia Lombardo. I was born on July 6, 2010, in the Micheal Garron hospital in East York, Ontario. I'm of Korean and Italian descent, and I live in Woodbridge with my mom, dad, and my cat Jake.

I play piano, and I just passed my RCM (Royal Conservatory of Music) grade 3 exam. I really like talking, piano, reading, writing and watching YouTube. I want to be a Microbiologist when I grow up because I want to try and create a cure for cancer.

I'm a huge anime fan, and my favourite anime/anime games are Danganronpa, Doki Doki Literature Club, Kakegurui, and The Promised Neverland. I also love to read, and my favourite book series are Harry Potter, Big Nate, and Jon le Bon. I really enjoy babysitting kids because I have a lot of younger cousins that I take care of. I also excel at swimming, and I just recently passed level 10. I can see myself becoming a lifeguard or a swimming instructor someday in the next few years.

I enjoy travelling, and I've been to Korea, Mexico, and Florida. I hope to travel to different parts of the world in the future. Right now my dream destination is Japan because it's the anime capital of the world.

Instragram: https://www.instagram.com/oliiveoilll/

STARTING FROM ROCK BOTTOM

MichaelNoble Emeghara

I know how it feels to be judged by others before they truly know me. I had a terrible experience where I was humiliated by a lecturer at the University Of Nigeria Nsukka (Alvan Campus) in the classroom when I tried to inquire about practical truth to contribute to the growth of others. Well, I asked the lecturer, "How could we apply Economics to the Nigerian Economy to increase our national position?" but I was called loads of names like stupid, crazy and was told I must be mad.

I am from Ngor Okpala Imo state in Nigeria, born third in the family of Mrs. Comfort and Mr. Cyril Emeghara. I am the Founder of *"The Mind Arena Academy,"* an Economist, International Ambassador, Global Icon, International Speaker, #1 International Bestseller, Magnetic Entrepreneur Inc. Affiliate, Guinness World Record participant, history's first Mental Interviewer and TheMindGuru of the world. I am blessed to have Kelechi Emeghara and Nneoma Emeghara as my siblings. I am grateful to my mentors, Dr. Pravin Patel and Sarah Lee Mba and numerous coaches. My mission, passion and purpose is to inspire two billion sleeping lions with my story and help them to awaken the Lion within with a proven philosophy that says "The Mind Arena Faith Speaks Life."

Most of my coursemates mocked me, seeing the old clothes I was wearing and trying to figure out what was real and true. I am among those students that prefer learning and have a big dream to inspire the world. Before the mind arena came, I was a positive person that professed that I had the good things in life, like saying, "I AM A MILLIONAIRE, I AM WEALTHY," etc., but people laughed at me, seeing the clothes I wore were not expensive and that I couldn't even pay my school fees without my parent's help. That was a terrible experience for me.

On that day, the 3rd of August, 2017, I felt like I was beaten up by life. All I could do was travel home to my little village in Imo State, Nigeria and go to the humble church where I worship, called The Lord's Bride. There, I asked God the same question I had asked the lecturer after fasting for three entire days without tasting food or water. I nearly died on the last day, but I never gave up. After concluding the fast on August 6, I had a blessed assurance that my prayers were answered.

On August 7, 2017, at 12:00 midnight, an angel of God appeared to me and called my name, "MichaelNoble, I have a message for you to give to the world," said the angel. Friends, I wanted to run far away seeing this gigantic, light being with a sword and shield. While I was running, the angel told me to wait. Then I waited and developed the courage to come closer to him. Then that light being touched my head, and I felt so powerful in that dream. He said, "Your mission is simple." Then a board appeared from nowhere, and the angel was holding a golden pen in his hand.

He wrote on that board, "THE MIND ARENA FAITH SPEAKS LIFE." He said, "Go and search for the meaning of this, study it and become one with it. You will learn the remaining actions as you move on." Imagine an Economist going to learn about "The Mind Arena." Isn't that crazy? A 300 level student moving back to learn about "The Mind Arena!" That's very crazy in the sight of man but phenomenal in God's sight.

To make a long story short, this is how I started studying the super successful, even though I didn't really know how to do it. All I knew was "The Mind Arena Faith Speaks Life," and nothing else mattered to me.

I failed in my first "The Mind Arena Group" on WhatsApp, which had members on five different continents of the world due to my phone being stolen. I was robbed when I was travelling back to my village. I told one of the admins, and he told the members of The Mind Arena Group.

Then I was thinking about how to restructure The Mind Arena and not about my recent failure. In 2018, I bought a new phone, an F1 Tecno and went back to the group. I decided to put The Mind Arena on Facebook where I met my Rich Dad, Dr. Pravin Patel, who later taught me how to write a book using a WhatsApp live video. It was truly awesome. He later introduced me to New York Times Bestsellers like Uncle Raymond Aaron, the living angel, Serena Brown Travis, and Robert J. Moore, etc. He gave me access to be taught by the greatest speakers of all time.

It wasn't long before I met Sarah Lee MBA in the Twin Flame Community. She became my twin flame. Oh, what a woman! Then I connected with her and started what I was so passionate about, The Mind Arena Faith Speaks Life.

I was posting my quotes for almost two years on Facebook. I don't know where they all came from. All I know is I was focused on inspiring people.

Sarah Lee saw my dedication and genuineness and decided to introduce me to her friends worldwide and paid the fee for me to be coached by the Greatest Speaker of All Time and also introduced me to Eric Zuley, who gave me access to meet his superstar celebrity friends in The EzWay TV Group on Facebook where I was recognized by two time Grammy Award Winner, Joel Diamonds. What a love. What a mother. This is how Sarah and Dr. Pravin Patel's influence led to my success in personal development. I will be discussing more of this in my upcoming book "*Rich Mum Rich Son, and Rich Dad Rich Son.*"

Watching my background and story will help you realize that you cannot judge a book by its cover. Judging where I came from, Umuoye Imerienwe Ngor Okpala Local Government Area of Imo state, the occupation there is mainly subsistence farming. This is a locality where the politicians are viewed almost as gods and the people their slaves, filled with inferiority complexes, low self-esteem and poor self-image. Yet, I still achieved greatness by writing this chapter in this book after being insulted, humiliated and embarrassed by the lecturer at the University Of Nigeria Nsukka (Alvan Campus).

Keys That Helped Create My Story

Belief

William James said, "*Believe and it will help create the fact.*" Yes, it's true. I stopped seeing the world as a big thing that is rotating in space and started seeing it as a tiny ball rolling inside the mind arena of living souls. We need to change our belief system and our mindigms. Mindigms are to me habits we develop from infancy to adulthood. When we reprogram our minds,we can reprogram our lives. This is why I say an abundant mind brings with it an abundant life.

Mentorship

For anyone to achieve greatness in life, you must first off be careful who your mentors are and how to deal with your mentors. It is said your income in the next five years will be the average of your friend's income.

Books

Books have been very important in my journey. I read 312 books in order to change my lifestyle and mentality, and stopped watching T.V. for eight years. It wasn't easy because some books I read were a Pdf; others were physical copies like *Think and Grow Rich*, *See You At The Top*, *The Richest Man In Babylon*, *The Magic Of Believing*, and *Power Of Awareness* by Neville Goddard, etc.

Seminars

I attended seminars organized by incredible people in the world that are my mentor's friend's seminars, and it was truly beautiful. They held them in a rural environment where people were busy discussing problems and Economic Meltdown. What I figured out is that our mentality is developed as we attend seminars organized by the greats. They affect our energy level, thereby bringing lasting impressions and great relationships as we network with those in attendance.

Willingness To Learn

You must be willing to learn and grow by opening up your mind to new wisdom and knowledge from your coaches. In order to become a Legend and Genius, you must, first of all, learn from those that are a Legend or a Genius. This is what I did. I told my friends and family that I didn't want to hear anything except from those that are a Legend or a Genius. I wanted to control my world and not allow others to do that for me. So I was willing to change and willing to learn new things too.

Relationships

My attitude toward myself manifested in my life. William James said, *"Human beings can change their lives by altering their attitude of mind."* I changed my attitude by first developing great relationships with myself and my Rich parents, Dr. Pravin Patel and Sarah Lee Mba. We need to have self-respect, self-value and self-worth. This will truly help us to achieve greatness in life.

Humility

I decided to put this at the end for a reason. Humility is often seen as a weakness, but friend, it is your greatest strength. John Ruskin said, *"The test of a great person is humility. When we become humble, our lives become a message to our generation."* This is a virtue most of the great people I've studied have; no matter their achievements, they are still willing to learn and grow to greater heights. They don't say they know it all; rather, they are open to new knowledge and wisdom from their mentors.

If you can adopt the lessons from my story, you will achieve greatness in life. *"The illiterates of our society will not be those that didn't go to school rather those that failed to use the mind technology given to mankind by the maker."* MichaelNoble, TheMindGuru.

An abundant mind brings with it an abundant life.

MichaelNoble Emeghara

MichaelNoble, TheMindGuru, is an author, Peace Ambassador, poet, 2x Celebrity Award Winning International Speaker and Guinness World Records participant, and 2x Celebrity Award Winning International Speaker, and the first person in African history to win three international public speaking awards on the same day, and is a life long learner.

He is The World Peace Ambassador to Canada and the United Kingdom, under Her Royal Majesty Queen of Africa, Queen Uba Iwunwa. He claims he is history's first mental interviewer after mentally interviewing 100+ of the greatest speakers.

His mission, vision and purpose is to awaken the greatness within you.

MichaelNoble can be reached at:

emegharamichaelnoble@gmail.com

ACCEPTANCE

Rev. Charmaine Lee, CHt

Acceptance is a difficult practice to maintain because there is a thought process. The thought process is an accumulation of stories and experiences that are connected to our beliefs. This is dependent upon how one has been raised within their family foundation. Sometimes it is cultural or the circumstances around their habitat. There are considerations to observe or understand. Nothing is just black and white.

The major issues that are restrictive for most women are the beliefs about being a woman. It is where strong expectations to uphold customary socio-ethnic appearances are passed down from generation to generation. The probability of the woman's role is perplexing as a mother, grandmother, a wife, a sister, a daughter, a professional, etc.

Women today face complicated concerns in the countless roles they play. Each hat worn becomes a new challenge. Often times this can trigger perfection that stops us from accepting our abilities. What happens is our self-preservation to look good or be good enough becomes a relentless competition.

For me, success is weighted upon my perfection to become the best, if not better, than I am now. I find myself rapidly running in a hamster wheel to catch up with others. As I reflect, I know many who have gone on to accomplish their dream(s). Instantly, it diminishes all that I have accomplished throughout my life. I begin to feel my successes are not enough. Why? What causes this to happen?

As I analyze this, I can hear the echoes within my mind as to what could I have done to be more successful. Instantly it triggers many questions provoking doubt. Why did I react so quickly, contradicting all that I accomplished? I thought all my hard work was enough. This only initiates my desire to have more. However, is it a desire to have success, or is it living my dream? My achievements should be gratifying. My need to be perfect manifests as I conclude, in my mind, I failed. Why am I judging myself so harshly?

Again, perfection raised its ugly head. Perfection is an addiction to want to be right or good. How is this so? I was taught during my childhood to satisfy an expectation of my parent's strong beliefs. It was an emotional competition where I competed with being good enough. Yes, being the eldest of four other siblings was a huge factor in my drive to be accepted. Everything became a burden upon me to succeed, which included taking care of my siblings. I had to balance all that I did with responsibility and fulfill an expectation of perfection. Today, it continually repeats this cycle where I have to literally remind myself to get off the spinning wheel.

Stop and think for a moment. I know you each can relate to this yearning of being accepted. It doesn't matter if you are at home, work, amongst your friends, your family; there is a strong desire to be accepted. Here is a metaphor. You are invited to attend your friend's birthday party, and you just found out a famous person will be there. We all react differently to this. How we dress, what our hair looks like, our shoes; you get the picture. Ultimately, we want to look good or impressive. Why? Are we judging ourselves against the famous person and his opinion of us?

How far does this addiction to be perfect or good enough continue? I ask myself this all the time. This does affect everything I do with the decisions I make, which can sometimes be damaging. I ffind myself driven by impulsiveness. I don't want to not be part of something. My thoughts overwhelmed me about what opportunity I might miss out on. In consequence, it formed conflicting questions and doubts.

Actually, this type of thought process can subsequently destroy the value of who you are. You begin to drown within your own truth. Women are always working so hard to be better. However, there is a percentage of women who decide to settle and be comfortable. This is hard work because the battle to fulfill everyone's expectations at times can be defeating. It is easier to surrender. "Why make waves?" Are we judging ourselves and thinking we are not capable? In that moment, it becomes a question of "Am I good enough" if I don't follow through. There are times women will tend to avoid a situation or pretend it didn't happen. We begin to justify.

In today's world, there exists a continuous battle for instant gratification. The urge to be important or recognized begins to grow. I have to do this now! Whatever it takes as the serotonin kicks in with our excitement. However, it is a temporary fix because the self-judgment of who you are is strong. One rush of not being enough can deter our focus. Instantly it becomes a conscious reality when our action falters. You begin to feel many thoughts and beliefs start to permeate your self-confidence.

Sounds ridiculous doesn't it? However, there is a simple resolution that everyone can identify with. It begins with acceptance. Acceptance is to love who you are. This must be the foundation to whether any self-judgment to be perfect is warranted.

How do we stop this progression? Because I wear many hats, all my thoughts collide with my beliefs, causing me to wrestle back and forth with my emotions and the battle with my mind. Logically, I can filter out the differences except when I begin to consider past experiences of my failures as my identity. It is like a loudspeaker within me repeatedly blasting that I will not succeed. Then I can see these flashcards in front of me showing me why I would not be accepted by anyone no matter what I do. I had become the inner critic, always judging myself negatively.

You see, part of my history has to do with being abused from the time I was conceived, the imprint of not being wanted and, as a child, I was not accepted. There were many beliefs as I was growing up. For one, the abuse did not stop at the first experience; it seemed to continue into my adulthood. Emotional, physical, mental and verbal abuse was the conduit to my own identity. Violence was incorporated into the mix where I lost my self-esteem. A victim of abuse became a label. There were people who got to know me and immediately ended the relationship as if I was a leper. The judgment didn't stop. It was evident that I was judged not only by my financial wealth, my appearance, my education but also by a label. It was a constant reminder embedded into my DNA. A definite battle as I had to fight constantly to learn to accept who I have become and love myself.

We all have our experiences through our thoughts and beliefs. However, you are not alone. The truth is we are not exempt from thought processes; therefore, no one is perfect. Each one of you has the ability to reason using your thought process to change. This is through acceptance of self.

You may feel insulted by this comment. There is no such thing as perfect! It is perfectly alright to be an imperfect human being. The truth is our imperfections are what make us perfect. Acceptance of self is the key to existence.

It isn't the abuse that created my identity. Abuse gave me the strength and focus to change a characteristic that is typically passed on from one generation to another. In spite of this, I did not let this be a benchmark in my life. Instead, I chose to take control of my conflicts and not be driven by reaction.

I love the quote from a commercial, "Don't hate me because I am beautiful"! When I decided to accept the person who I was and not the label, it was an alternative to begin to love who I am. Our past never defines who we are. As a woman, I have to decide to treat myself every day as a unique individual. Every one of us should execute this practice.

It is a natural evolution to want to be the best you can be. I found that through abuse, I lost more than an identity. I did not accept myself as long as I had to be perfect. The best way to begin is to start treating yourself as a unique individual. You have the ability to reason and can make a choice because free will can change the course of your direction. First, you must find a place to start, and that is through acceptance. Acceptance is the key to open up to loving oneself and to cast out the desire for perfection.

Accept where you are in your life. It is the only way you know where you are going. If it isn't where you want to go, you can change it. Accept who you are today. If you don't like who you have become, then it is up to you to take responsibility to improve upon who you are. It begins with being truthful with yourself and loving yourself enough to decide what you want.

Charmaine Lee

Charmaine Lee is certified in many aspects of personal growth. She is currently assisting others as a Communication Specialist, Life Coach, Author, and Inspirational Speaker. Her expertise as an Integrative NLP (Neurolinguistic) Master Practitioner, Personal Empowerment Trainer, and certified Metaphysician is diverse. She has spoken to audiences in person, via virtual networks, and through television interviews. She spoke as keynote speaker for a variety of groups, especially for S.A.F.E. House in Las Vegas, Nevada, an organization for which she is passionate.

In 2013, Charmaine's first book was released, "Gardenias Bruise Easily, Giving Silence a Voice from Abuse to Love," which is about her search for truth. Her silence, withholding anger, and abuse were destroying her own personal power. The battle within her consciousness formed a barrier when it came to her success.

In addition, Ms. Lee has contributed to numerous books as a co-author for self-help, personal awareness, and leadership. She is personally working on two more books about empowerment and self-preservation.

Charmaine's desire to help people extended into working for the L.A. County Sheriff's and the Las Vegas Metropolitan Police Department for 18 years sequentially. It was through these agencies where she began to volunteer in multiple roles to make a difference for those who were in trauma, children in need, and women/men of domestic violence. She was proactive in assembling assistance to all socio-ethnic groups of all ages within the community.

Charmaine Lee studied under Dr. Ken Fabian, an expert in human behavior. This kindled her determination to 'go deeper'. It led her to offer personal development to adults and children. She was able to offer her services as the Director of YMCA working with youths in the outreach areas. Inspired, Charmaine developed fundamental tools for individuals to use as a self-guided practice for self-help. Later, she integrated a communication tool called, BANKCODE into a program she developed, "Mindful Success Systems," as a compilation of tools for empowerment.

www.charmaine-lee.com

www.atomy.com/us/home

BELIEVE YOUR SELF-WORTH

Jennifer Woodbeck Thompson

When I look back at my childhood, I picture many laughs and fun times camping with my parents and sister, trips with our extended family, swimming in the backyard, but when I picture my friends, there are moments that I feel insecure and sad. My memories as a child are great, and I had amazing friends, some of whom I am still extremely close with today, yet I still feel a pit in my stomach for some of the moments that defined when I felt not good enough or felt tragic in my soul. I remember sitting in the schoolyard the first day of school when someone told me my legs were fat, which seems so ridiculous to me now, but at the time, I wished a hole would open in the earth and suck me in. I remember feeling this many more times and wishing that the hole would appear again. The vision of the hole opening and sucking me in has helped me through many shameful moments in life or what I felt were shameful.

When I first started my career as a Respiratory Therapist (RT), I believed I was capable of being the best for my patients, but in my first job at the Sick Children's Hospital, I was quickly put down and told I didn't know anything. For the first time in my life, I couldn't make friends, and I was in an environment where people didn't believe I could do many things. I tried to find ways to learn more, ask more questions, and build friendships, but each time I tried, I was put down, ignored, and told I didn't know anything. It was a hard environment to be in when I had always found making friends easy. After a few months, I made the decision that the environment wasn't the best for me and thought about quitting, but I knew I would feel like a failure. This was my first job after graduating, and I couldn't cut it. Well, as luck would have it, I didn't get to make the decision to quit because I was fired. I WAS FIRED! I couldn't believe it; I hadn't been fired from anything before, I never failed at anything before, I never felt so embarrassed before. I was devastated and didn't know where to turn. Luckily, I had made some great friends in school, and when I told them what happened, I quickly got a phone call from another hospital offering me a temporary contract. I was afraid to say yes because I wasn't sure if I would be capable of being a Respiratory Therapist, but I feared the lack of money to pay bills more, so I said yes. My experiences at Mount Sinai Hospital were phenomenal. My confidence grew as I trained with some of the most amazing RTs and learned so much. I still had moments that I doubted my abilities, but I learned to ask for help, and with the help, I gained confidence.

I had many occurrences of doubting my abilities throughout my career in healthcare, and the image of a hole continued each time I felt that doubt. Over time, I learned to be what I call a "Cameleon." I learned to smile and adapt to all situations. I learned to say the right thing and tell stories that are relatable to what others are telling me. I learned how to politely mirror and mimic the people around me so that I would be liked, relatable and loved. We all want to be liked and loved, but there are times when we feel our self-worth is dependent on what others believe we are. That is one of the hardest life cycles we put ourselves through, believing our self-worth is based on what others think of us.

I began to find more of my self-worth when I allowed myself to see who I am through my husband's eyes. My husband is my biggest fan and always believed that I could do amazing things, even when I may not. It wasn't always easy to accept his compliments and praise, and at times I would turn him away or seem annoyed because I wasn't ready to see what he saw.

A lot of my lack of confidence changed when I finally left the healthcare environment after 17 years of work. Don't get me wrong; it is not a bad place to work. Helping people is a mission I hold dear to my heart, but in the healthcare environment, there is underfunding, understaffing, and a hierarchy of people that are primarily looking for the negative things you do rather than praising you for a job well done. But I was lucky. Lucky enough to find a mission and a passion that would still help people but in a positive and hopeful way. I changed the life of my family by becoming a financial professional.

Becoming a financial professional was much easier than I had ever believed. I was introduced to the new profession by two wonderful women who also had a mission and vision larger than themselves. They taught me to believe that I was amazing! We shared leadership and leaned on each other when needed, but we never judged one another. I learned to read books differently, find inspiration differently, and find ways to reward myself and others for the small successes in life. Not only did my career change, but my heart, body, and soul also changed. These women also learned how to properly value people because their leadership also taught them those skills. I am truly blessed to have been introduced to World Financial Group because the company puts value in growing people into leaders and helps celebrate all the small wins you have in business. When I compare my two careers, the only time I heard from a healthcare manager/director was when I was disciplined, whereas now, when I hear from leadership, it is to provide support and congratulations. Tell me what that does for your self-worth!

There is a saying, *"You are the average of the five people you spend the most time with"* - Jim Rohn, and that couldn't be truer. When I look at my life, I realize that I am a product of my environment. From my childhood experiences until recently, I based my self-worth on what others around me felt about me. Don't get me wrong, on occasion, I fall back to the failures in my head that pick at me to tell me that I am not enough, but now I can easily see myself as my husband sees me.

I believe we all have a choice in life to fall into that hole in the earth or find a new path around it. I still have my moments of doubt, but I look at each not as a failure but as an opportunity to learn something new and find more self-worth. I believe I can succeed at anything! Now, as an adult, I have enough self-confidence to share with the world, and you can too. If you ever doubt your self-worth, find your people that see you as bigger and better than you see yourself; you deserve it!

Jennifer Woodbeck Thompson

Jennifer Woodbeck Thompson is the consummate financial professional. Not only does she provide the full spectrum of financial products and services, as well as knowledgeable advice, she is also an in-demand speaker and a published author. Jennifer is your Friendly Finance Coach, based in Mississauga, Ontario, and has clients throughout North America.

As a Financial Professional, Jennifer has the unique ability to service her clients as a finance coach, helping them better understand their personal money beliefs, insights into budgeting and tracking, strategies to help them become more financially successful, as well as educating on basic financial concepts. Jennifer also has the luxury of working with one of the largest insurance and investment brokers, World Financial Group. Jennifer offers and advises on a full range of services offered by over 50 financial services companies. Her services include Retirement Planning; Debt Management; Savings and Investments; Life, Critical Illness and Disability Insurance; Estate Planning; and Tax saving strategies. Her particular focus is currently on ensuring her clients will be financially stable in the event of unexpected healthcare challenges. After her years in the medical field, she understands that not everything is covered when a medical emergency arises, and the financial repercussions can be long-lasting.

Expanding on her work in financial services, Jennifer has turned to the idea of educating people on the importance of managing their financial picture. To that end, she works one-on-one with her clients, doing regular check-ins on their current situations and managing any changes as they arise. She is also doing financial education webinars and speaking at events in the US and Canada. She is an award-winning and best-selling author of *"Butterflies and Shiny Things: A Women's Guide on How to Manage Financial Distractions."*

"Change is good. Just have a plan."

Jennifer Woodbeck Thompson
Financial Professional
President, Friendly Finance Coach
friendlyfinacecoach@gmail.com
647-949-1099

CHALLENGE YOURSELF

Preston Woodbeck

Once upon a time, there was a young redheaded boy, his name was Preston Woodbeck. He was interested in soccer and lots of other sports, but he loved soccer more than anything. Well, that's not really true; he also really liked playing video games, but that meant he was inside, so outside, he loved to play soccer. His favourite video games were Brawlhalla and Fortnite. Anyway, back to the story, Preston loves to play soccer. He started playing soccer at the age of four, and at seven, tried out for a competitive soccer team in Thunder Bay. The soccer team was called the Thunder Bay Chill. The team was good enough to travel to tournaments in the United States of America for the USA Cup and Winnipeg for the Golden Boy tournament. The USA Cup is the largest youth international soccer tournament with 1,152 teams from 22 U.S. states and 20 countries.

In 2019 Preston had to move from Thunder Bay to Mississauga since his dad was getting transferred. Initially, Preston was really disappointed because he would miss his school friends and soccer friends, but Preston hoped he could go back to see his friends sometime again. Preston was sad but also knew he would make new friends in Mississauga, where he was moving.

When Preston moved, his mom tried to find a team that would take him mid-way through the season, so he practiced with a soccer team for REP. It was a really crappy soccer team because they didn't allow Preston to show his skills and didn't make him feel like part of the team. When it was time for tryouts, the coaches held two days of tryouts and then kept the people that were already on the team and told everyone else that they didn't need anyone new! Preston didn't feel very good about himself for not making the team. He felt like they were judging him even before they got to know his skills.

Preston decided to just play house league instead of competitive soccer, so he found a new league to go to so he wouldn't have to see any of the other players from the REP team. It was fun again! After a summer of house league Preston found he liked soccer again and wanted to try out for the competitive Erin Mills Eagles. Preston was really nervous to go to the soccer tryouts; he even doubted himself! There were some people who doubted he would make the tryouts for his soccer team, including himself! He then told them and himself that he was going to make the team, so he made an incredible decision. He kicked the soccer ball from a corner kick with the plan to place it in front of the soccer net. He got ready for the kick, told himself he could do it, and then he made the kick. The soccer ball landed just on top of the soccer net instead of in front of it, but it gave him the ability to show the coaches that he would be good for the team. No other kids could kick the soccer ball like Preston. He successfully made the team!!

For the first few months on his new team, Preston was really excited to see his new teammates and learn to play soccer with them. The team was a pretty decent team. There were many players, so the team was divided into two teams, the attacking team and the defending team. The coaches arranged it so that the better players were on the attacking team and the newer players were on the defending team. Preston was kind of mad because he was put on the defending team, but Preston didn't give up; he worked hard and learned fast. The team had many new players, so they were pretty bad and lost most of the games in the first season. There were also some players that thought they were the best but who didn't have the competitive training and experience that Preston did. Those players didn't think Preston was very good and would yell at him to make different gameplays than what he was taught. The coaches stepped in and helped those players understand they weren't the best and that they all needed to play as a team. That made Preston feel better about himself as a soccer player also because he knew he understood the game of soccer differently and had better skills than the other players, even if they didn't see it in him yet. Isn't it strange how they judged Preston without knowing his skill level?

In 2020 COVID affected soccer, and all the teams had to start practicing online on zoom videos. UGH! Preston and his teammates didn't like soccer on zoom because it was painful not doing it with other teammates. When the next outdoor season came, the team was able to practise outside, but everyone was not ready because barely anyone participated in the soccer zoom meetings, so they didn't understand what the coaches wanted. Preston even wanted to quit! But his mom told him to participate in the first couple of practices and if he still wanted to quit, then he could. He started to go to every practice, and at every practice, Preston didn't give up. He tried and tried and kept pushing to become the best on his team. Preston didn't give up, and so far this season, he won a couple of games. That is an improvement! At times, Preston believed what other people told him about himself, so much so, that he was almost going to give up soccer. But Preston learned that with a little bit of belief in himself and telling himself that he was a good soccer player, he was able to be the best player on his team!

Preston Woodbeck

"When the going gets tough, the tough play soccer"

Preston Woodbeck is a strong, fired-up 13-year-old who loves testing the limits in all things.

Preston mainly throws himself into soccer and video games. He was born five weeks early and struggled in his first few years with repeated hospital admissions and at one point was thought to have cystic fibrosis. But the passion inside Preston never dulled.He started downhill skiing at the age of two and learned to swim on his own by the age of three. By the time Preston was four years old, he had grown taller than most of the kids his age and found a passion for soccer. Any piece of paper, ball, or rock became his soccer ball, and he would kick it with fierce precision. He tried out for the Thunder Bay Chill competitive soccer team at the age of seven and started training regularly. Preston travelled to soccer tournaments throughout Canada and the US with his teammates to play against kids from around the world. Over the past few years, he has moved cities and found an interest in video games during the COVID lockdown but he is very happy to be playing soccer again with the Erin Mills Eagles. Preston always looks for the good in everyone and helps others be successful and feel encouraged.

Preston has a passion for everything he does and puts his full heart into being successful.

Youtube: PrestonROXX

https://www.youtube.com/channel/UCE2LYH9Wbh1OQ B4Kz7T1XYA/featured

PEOPLE BELIEVE WHAT THEY WANT TO BELIEVE

Denise C. Nadeau

"Don't judge a book by its cover" is an idiom that's probably been used since books began; however, the first documented reference dates to 1860. It was later publicized in a murder mystery novel in 1946, and is now a common phrase, in some form, in most languages. Its meaning is simple: one should not judge the worth or value of something by its outward appearance alone. A similar phrase is "all that glitters is not gold." The concept was a crucial element in the teachings of Jesus as referenced in The Bible. "Judge not, lest ye be judged." It seems an important subject to contemplate.

To judge something or someone is extremely uncomfortable for me. In the past, I have been on the receiving end of judgement, and it has a deeply disturbing effect on the psyche, and it is incredibly frustrating. Especially when the judgement is 100% false. That is when perception comes into play. You need to understand that a person's perception IS their reality, and what they believe to be true is, in fact, true to them.

My personal story about being judged.

It's only one of many. I worked for a company for at least 7 years when I was in my late 20's to early 30's. I had moved back to Houston after being away for 10 years in Austin, Texas. So, I wasn't exactly connected with friends from my high school days. I felt completely isolated and was starting over. A co-worker, a man 20+ years my senior, took an interest in me and we became friends. We were both single, not in a relationship, and we soon discovered we enjoyed many of the same activities. We had an understanding between us that we were meant to be "great friends," but it was mutually agreed that we were not meant to be romantically involved. And there <u>was not</u> any fooling around going on.

However, most of our co-workers perceived and concluded that because we spent so much time together there HAD to be a romantic connection. Regardless of how many times we reiterated that we were strictly friends, no one ever believed us. "You must be trying to keep it a secret," we were told. And there wasn't a damn thing we could do to convince them otherwise.

By the way, the reason we maintained a friendship status was because I was young and still had hopes of having a marriage and family, and he wasn't interested in having more children at his age. To this day, those co-workers still believe something false was true.

Is all judgement considered bad?

What about positive judgement that is intended to praise someone or something? The problem with judgement in general is that it sets a level of expectation, whether positive or negative. Both the judger and the judged can be hurt in the process. Consider this scenario: your boss judges you to be the model employee, one whom everyone should strive to emulate. She or he is often singing your praises to the rest of the staff. To your extreme misfortune, one day you make a mistake or act out of character. Imagine that you accidentally overslept the morning an important meeting was scheduled with a highly desired client who could potentially double your company's sales and revenue. In other words, a really big fish. And YOU were charged with making the presentation and closing the deal.

You worked diligently into the early morning hours to fine-tune the proposal to the point of perfection. In this state of sleep deprivation, you accidentally slept through the alarm on this critical day and missed the meeting altogether. BIG MISTAKE! You are only human, after all, and everyone makes mistakes, right? How do you imagine your boss is feeling because of your mistake?

Well, unless your boss is named Jesus, she or he is most likely feeling extremely disappointed and let down. Not just with you, but with him or herself, too. They are now wondering "how could they have been so wrong and misjudged you in the first place?" They now have a new judgment of you: unreliable and disappointing. What's more, it is highly unlikely they will change their new opinion of you and your character.

Can you now see how judgement can hurt everyone? A positive judgement can flip to a negative one in a heartbeat and is likely to remain so. The same is true of an instantaneous negative judgement, which is likely to stick unless some miracle is performed, or an act of God proves it to be a misjudgment. Most people simply don't like to admit they are wrong.

Some people will not like you, and it's not your fault!

Let's face it, not everyone loves or even likes certain people based on a trait or characteristic they seem to embody. Some people do judge others for any and every reason imaginable. Perhaps you remind them of someone who betrayed them, or you are too loud or too quiet. The list goes on, and you may never know the reason why you rub someone the wrong way. Even worse is someone who pretends to like you when the opposite is true. How does one ever know who is trustworthy when they are unwilling to be honest? I would rather know that a person did not like me so I could stop participating in a dramatic ruse and looking like a fool.

Passing judgement: we all do it, but can we stop?

The simple answer is yes, but not without concerted effort and mindfulness. Making changes within our mind is a skill and it takes practice. Observe or monitor your thoughts, ideally always, but at the very least as often as you can. I know it sounds like an impossible undertaking, but it's critical if you intend to make a change.

Remember, thoughts are things, and you should be questioning your internal dialogue to determine what is valid and what should be rejected or corrected. Some thoughts do tell you lies which you begin to internalize and believe to be true. So, it just makes sense that we examine and challenge the validity of the thoughts running amuck in our head.

When you catch yourself passing judgement, immediately interrupt that thought with a resounding STOP! Just imagine a big stop sign has jumped in front of you and refuses to allow your thought to continue. Then gently remind yourself of your intention to stop being judgmental.

Understanding...

The next step is to try and put yourself in their shoes. Whether you want to admit it or not, we are all human beings designed from the same material. Every one of us can do the things we humans will do. Good and bad. The homeless person living under the bridge probably didn't start out there. Somewhere along the way, they either made poor choices, caught a tough break, lost a job, became disabled or are simply suffering from unfortunate circumstances beyond their control.

Millions of people in this country live paycheque to paycheque and have little to zero money in a savings account. They have nothing to fall back on and keep afloat should the dreaded, unexpected, incapacitating event arrive on their doorstep. Now imagine that happening to you. How much time will you have before the mortgage company forecloses on your house or the landlord comes with an eviction notice? How long will you be able to put food on the table to feed your family?

Eventually, you will find yourself in line at the government social services building applying for assistance and food stamps. Where will you and your family live? In a shelter if you're lucky or perhaps under a bridge if you're not. No one is immune to this unwelcomed tumble into poverty. Not even the wealthy. You've heard the "rags to riches" story, but there is an alternative story on the flip side of that coin, which is "insanely wealthy to immediate bankruptcy and broke." Bad things happen to good people all the time, and you are no exception.

Acceptance...

Once you realize that you too could be that homeless person living under the bridge, the next step is acceptance. This step is easy, as it does not require any action or effort on your part. All you need to do is accept that person just as they are. Apply that principle to everyone you encounter because one brief glance or meeting will never give you insight into the totality of the life they have lived to this point. Just be willing to give the gift of non-judgement.

There is nothing to fix here because you don't have the power to change anyone other than yourself. Do you believe in God or a higher power? If so, then you might understand this concept. You (your soul) and your higher power agreed that you needed more work in a particular area and designed a life of specific circumstances and challenges that will enable you to achieve a deeper understanding. It is not your job to interfere with or entangle yourself in what another person came here to achieve, especially since you are not privy to the agreement or their life's purpose.

What's the point?

Exactly! What IS the point to relieve yourself from the burden of judging someone or something? Love is the answer. Every one of us is both loveable AND unlovable at times. This is the duality of the world we live in and the law of nature. Light and dark, open and closed, past and future.

Furthermore, people will believe what they want to believe, and they don't often like to admit they were wrong. So, setting out to change someone's opinion of you is futile.

In fact, it's not your job to do so! What others think of you, quite frankly, is none of your business. You must accept, for your own sanity, that you are powerless to change another person. You are in charge of only you.

Quit trying to win some imaginary popularity contest! Honestly, you will have just as many people who are not your fans as you will have admirers. Don't take it personally, and don't get stuck trying to figure out <u>why</u>.

What matters is what YOU think of YOU. Focus your energy on more meaningful and creative endeavours that bring you joy. Understanding, accepting, love and joy are effortlessly passed from one to another. Doesn't everyone need more of that in their lives?

"To thine own self be true." William Shakespeare

Denise C. Nadeau

Denise has 25+ years of experience as a business office administrator in a variety of industries. She is well-known for her exceptional variety of talent and is never one to set limits on her potential.

As an entrepreneur, she is an established voice-over actor with multiple audiobooks and commercials to her credit and a network marketing professional in the health and wellness industry.

Other interests include creative writing, scuba diving, and travel. She admits that she was "born to cruise," as she finds tranquility being surrounded by water.

Denise currently resides in Houston, Texas.

To reach her, check out her websites:

www.goodbodyhealing.com

www.denisevoactor.com

or email at dee13tx@gmail.com

EVERYONE HAS A STORY, IT'S IN THE DETAILS YOU DISCOVER THEIR GIFTS

Gabrielle McKenna

Speaking of being judgmental, have you noticed how disrespectful and presumptuous some people have become, especially these past few decades with regard to our elders? Movements like "kids got rights" and "it's not our fault" teach our youth today to cast blame, be lazy and not to appreciate the value and impact our seniors/parents have made in our lives.

One senior that has made an impact on me is my dad. My dad is a retired high school teacher. He taught chemistry, computer science and coached soccer. While he was strict and a disciplinarian, he also had a good sense of humour, loved the outdoors and would go out of his way to encourage and support his students. Some students would later recall how his life's teachings helped them as they became adults.

In our home, being the eldest of four girls, he was even more strict with me as he believed I was "carving the path" for my sisters. Consequently, I left home in my final year of high school. I now realize the person I am today is because of my dad. My dad is a person of his word; he is reliable and hardworking. He will go out of his way to help and contribute. He believes in education and always encouraged me to be open to receiving a new idea or thought.

He did his very best in every moment. Most of all, he showed me that doors will open when you are polite and respectful and lead with integrity, value and heart.

This year (Sept 2021), my dad turned 82. He is a triple bypass (1996) and a myeloma cancer survivor. Since Dec 2016, he has undergone three separate chemo treatments and, as recently as the summer of 2020, 15 rounds of back-to-back radiation for his cancer. I am very grateful he is still with us.

In the early morning of March 09, 2017, the effects of one of the chemo treatments took my dad's life. Whilst prepping for his morning shave from his seated walker, he collapsed to the washroom floor. Between frantic tears coupled with my mother's relentless chest-pounding while screaming, "Wake up Mac, Mac wake up!" it took what seemed minutes before dad was brought back to consciousness and then taken away by ambulance to the hospital.

It is believed, during this brief death encounter, my dad suffered some cognitive brain damage which has subsequently made him lose confidence in some of his abilities.

To look at my father, you will see a frail man alone with a drink in hand whilst sitting in front of his Smart TV or laptop in silence, often in deep thought. Dad has a way of seeing life and believes everyone should be contributing to the betterment of the cause. He has no tolerance for people who do not add value to life and/or community and is very direct when communicating his thoughts on paper that many of his commentaries have been published.

When given the opportunity, he is happy to share his thoughts because this makes him feel valued even though each passing day sees him getting less confident and more dependent. Today, simple tasks quickly tire him; joys like washing his vehicles, small home maintenance and repairs, grocery shopping, helping my mum entertain and feed her art students, going out for country drives and travelling with my mum to see friends and family have become cumbersome.

Behind his thick spectacles are signs of advanced cataracts, and while he has lost 70%+ of his hearing, he is finding it difficult to interact in settings where these senses are most needed; therefore chooses to stay in the confines of his basement. For most people, hearing aids is a sensible auxiliary, however like me, dad's ear canals are very small, making these aids difficult to properly stay secured in the canals. Consequently, conversations are repeated often, voices are raised to the point tempers get short, leaving him questioning why people are yelling at him, which leaves him frustrated and short-tempered because the communications are misunderstood.

A typical day in my dad's life: He's up, showered and dressed by 9-9:30 a.m. Mum's usually up between 4:30, and 6:00 a.m. and will check in from time to time to ensure he is still breathing. Once up, double Oxo hot bevy and maybe a bowl of porridge pre-prepped by my mum or Weetabix is consumed before taking his stair chair lift down to his open 1100+ sqft floor fully furnished walk-out bright windowed basement.

With a well-stocked bar, a big comfy chair that is positioned in front of a large gas fireplace topped by a not so

Smart large tele, while a few feet away positioned is his large cherrywood office desk and leather padded swivel office chair, a new large-screen laptop and printer await as dad preps his first drink before taking in the days news. On the same floor is a private double bedroom with a full washroom, a separate laundry room and mum's art studio.

I'm sure there are days when dad looks at those daunting stairs knowing one day he will have to resign himself to living permanently in this downstairs space. That's why, despite the number of drinks, his pride and fight to hold onto his independence still motive him to get in that chair and get up those stairs. Each night I am there, I am grateful I am able to provide reassurance he will safely make it up to my mother's side.

During the day, CP24 TV is muted in the background and online sites like the UK's Daily Mail, the Globe and Mail are dad's resources as he attempts to make sense of the chaos in the world. I see he can sense there's a shift taking place as he prepares his documents for my mum to eventually take over the household bills.

Simple joys like talking to his sisters and cousins on Skype, intermittent visits from my three sisters and his two grandchildren, along with me coming down with my two kittens every other week, help break up the routine. I believe the ability for my dad to continue to solve The Globe's daily cryptic crossword is his test to prove he is still of value.

Keeping on top of European Football gives him reason to converse with his grandson on their team, Man United knowing the torch will be continued when he is gone. Jamie

Oliver's latest meal prep menu reminds my dad of his laboratory days as spices like the periodic table must be carefully balanced to create the right experience.

As my dad gets fussier, more critical and more stubborn, I see my mum worry and be frustrated. I observe her silent tears as she comes to terms knowing her husband, my dad, may one morning or one afternoon not wake up.

I am reminded that life is so precious, and you've got to make the most of what is. That's why my mum needs an outlet – she relies on her tablet, coffee, lunch and retail therapy outings with the girls and her girl's visits to help her cope with the inevitable.

I've found that front porch sittings have provided great impromptu opportunities to help my dad to engage with the neighbours and get out of the basement. At the end of the day, even though my mother struggles to stay awake, my dad still prefers to sit by her side with either his arm around her or holding her hand as they sit on the couch watching an episode or two of *Escape to the Country*.

Then around 8:00 p.m. or so, my mum reminds my dad to print the next day's crypto puzzle and, once in hand, dad tops up his drink and joins my mum in bed where they work on a few of the answers before falling asleep. I notice more often that dad is getting up several times in the middle of the night as I wonder what items he still is reviewing to keep the smooth inevitable transition.

To know my younger dad, you would know him to have long days and late nights, typically marking his student's papers and or teaching night and summer school classes to earn enough income to support his wife and four children and upgrade his skillset. He rarely drank but loved to entertain with backyard campfires inviting our neighbours and their children to participate in sing-alongs and story-telling.

My dad also loved to tinker with cars, kept his cars very tidy, could be seen mending or making home improvements and always strived to do the best he could. His commitment to being the best version of himself, a good neighbour, being respectful to your elders, and an example for your children and students taught us you are bound not only by your word but your actions.

He is well-loved and respected. My dad is also a published author, has hob-knobbed with some of the world's elite and is happy to share those stories; he has rebuilt a life in four different countries and retired quite comfortably with the love of his life, my mother of 53 years.

Even though my dad's family was very poor and simple, he remains humble and extremely grateful for the life he has lived and built. He was born in Blackpool, England, in 1939, the only son and second child of four to Eileen and Leslie McKenna. When my dad was two, my grandfather, a plumber, enlisted and served four years in WWII to fight for the freedoms that are being attempted to be taken away today.

After the war, my grandfather was fortunate to return to his family to later meet his demise at age 54 from a similar heart attack and condition that my dad survived at age 56 due to the advancement of medicine.

My dad's uncles, three of my grandfather's siblings were law enforcement officers and inspectors, one of which helped track down and capture many of the Nazi criminals to bring them to justice. My dad is proud of his upbringing, the lessons and the people he has been fortunate enough to meet.

He knows the difference between right and wrong, is a man of his word and believes it is always better to do what is right even if it means the journey may take a little bit longer. The friendships he has acquired and the many he still maintains, one of which helped him receive the scholarship to St Andrews University in Scotland to give him an education in chemistry, physics and the biosciences that helped provide for his family and afford the lifestyle he enjoys today.

Next time you encounter a senior, remember every person has a story and gift despite their physical and or cognitive appearance. I encourage you to be open to receiving those gifts, especially when you see a senior sitting on their own, struggling to find change or just walking too slow in front of you. After all, one day, you will look back to realize you are now one.

Many blessings.

Gabrielle McKenna

Helping Families and Entrepreneurs Plan for the Unplanned. Live with Purpose, Passion and Fun!

Life throws you curves and Gabrielle has learned no matter what shows up, you discover a part within you that can pull through it and make you stronger, more intuitive and more open to receiving new ideas and insights.

As a licensed financial advisor, she helps individuals, families and entrepreneurs get organized, educated and gets cash flowing by implementing specific strategies to protect, manage and build their wealth so they can have the confidence, time and energy to enjoy life on their terms.

The best way to connect with her is
gabs360.com,
416-409-6914
gm4success@yahoo.ca

TWO FACES – LOVE VS. JUDGMENT

Nadira Dyalsingh

As I thought about this topic of *"Don't Judge a Book By Its Cover,"* I realized that this is a two-way street; sometimes I judge, and sometimes I am judged.

My first story to share with you goes back to 1992, when I first decided to emigrate to Canada. I had spent the previous twelve years studying and working in England with all intentions of spending the rest of my life there.

England was the dream country where I wanted to live. As a child in Guyana, formerly British Guyana, we got many of our foods and fruits from England. The Christmas cards had sparkles on pictures of families having fun in the snow. Our school examinations were sent from England.

Yes, I wanted to be Immersed in the culture. It didn't matter that the final six years, I lived in Whitechapel Methodist Mission, where the homeless or substance abusers would come for food, church, and health care. I occasionally assisted at the mission during my university days and was working as a Registered Midwife three doors away.

Then my parents decided to move from Guyana to Canada, from a tropical place to a place where it is cold almost six months of the year. I decided to move to Canada too, to assist my parents in settling there. I thought, "Oh, they speak English there, I will get a job easily." I did no research about life in Canada.

When I told my friends and relatives that I was moving to Canada, they were surprised, and to my dismay, they were really trying to discourage me. They said that I wouldn't like it, it's too cold. "Yes, it would be nice to be able to see your parents, but you won't get a job. The pace is too fast; you won't fit in. Oh! You won't last there; you'll be back soon. Don't take all your things with you because you won't stay. It is too expensive to live there. All your friends are here."

I was sad to hear all those negative comments. I felt that I was an adventurous person who enjoyed travelling and was now about to share life again with my parents in a new country. I spent six months in Canada before returning to Whitechapel. On my first day back, I met my midwifery instructor, Dora, and the next day I was back at work at the Royal London Hospital, and yes, once again living at Whitechapel Methodist Mission. Six months later, I packed my bags and returned to Canada, where I got my first job ten days later, and in 2021 I am still here!!

Yes, life in my new job was different; fear and anxiety filled many of my days as I recalled what my friends and relatives had told me in England. However, I wanted to be here with my parents. I still have strong friendships with those I left in England. They still talk about being surprised that I left and stayed away from England for such a long time. I had to learn new ways of working, and yes, the pace of life was faster but, I had to work and soon started caring for my ailing parents.

I am grateful for the "hands-on" nurses' training I got in England, but I built stamina and 'grit' for myself in Canada. I learned not only about being there for others but, being there for myself. In so doing, I have been able to find joy wherever I go. These days, my friends talk about my resilience.

Three years later, I chose to do a nursing placement by The University of Toronto in Northern Ontario, Canada. I had seen photographs of students in various nurses' stations in Northern Ontario, and they spoke of fishing, being at the lake after their daily shifts, beautiful northern lights, communal eating, and much more. I wanted that experience, but, once again, I did not do any research about living on Indigenous Reservations in Canada.

In April 1996, I left Toronto for Margaret Gray Nursing Station, Cat Lake Indian Reserve, Sioux Lookout, Ontario. I remember boarding Bearskin Airlines from Thunder Bay, and half an hour later, we were landing on what seemed like a pebble road in a forest. The airport was an empty wood hut next to an outhouse. A worker from the nurses' station met me there, and before leaving for the bumpy ride on the snowy mud road, he unplugged the landline telephone from the hut and carried it with him. The telephone was only taken there when they were expecting a plane to land. Plane landings there were few and far between.

The lake was frozen, with skidoo tracks everywhere. From one area which never freezes, the residents collected their water. The lake, forestry and golden sunshine scenery were beautiful. The homes with outhouses were log houses, wood or concrete.

On arrival at the station, I was asked to take my shoes off at the door. I never had to take off my shoes before entering a health facility but, there I did, and so did everyone else. Later, I was told that outdoor footwear stayed at the door for the cleanliness of the station. The staff wore different footwear inside the station, and the patients would keep on their socks.

Days and weeks went by, and I remained in awe at the poor living conditions of the residents. How could they not have running water or electricity, or indoor plumbing in their homes? When the snow began to melt, there was so much garbage on such a small piece of land. The children would play in the dirt and have fun catching tiny guppy fishes in the muddy streams. I saw that life there was hard, yet the people were so appreciative and humble. I met the founder of the Margaret Gray Nursing Station, Margaret Gray, a very inspiring person full of wise words.

Yes, I should have read about the culture of the Indigenous people. Once again, I took for granted that I would understand a new culture. I wondered why no one was looking at my face during a conversation. They would lower their eyes toward the floor with a slight downward tilt of their head. At first, I felt uncomfortable with no eye contact and thought it was rude, but later found out it was a sign of respect.

The winter months were harsh on the small island. School classes were up to grade 9. As the weeks went by, I found myself judging the people, asking why weren't they working, why didn't they eat vegetables? The veggies were all drying up in the one store which sold everything needed on the island. I asked myself many "whys."

I began to equate their poor living conditions and physical appearance with lower education. But, as I met more and more of the residents, I began to realize how wrong I was.

I was amazed at their incredible memory. They remembered in detail all their medications, new ones, old ones, doses, frequencies, negative and positive reactions, colours and shapes of the medications, and names of the doctors who attended to them (one doctor visits every three months).

They were so versed in health care and storytelling and making the best of what they had. It was so humbling and inspiring to be there. They appreciated all the care and loved to return favours with thanksgiving. Before I left Cat Lake, the ladies enjoyed roasting a duck outdoors and made moccasins and beaded jewellery for me to bring to Toronto. I returned their good wishes by sending them all the gifts they requested.

Their gratitude and humbleness in a very minimalistic lifestyle is so very rich and I am so grateful to have had the opportunity to be so inspired by those I felt were undereducated. Years later, I still have fond memories of the people of Cat Lake, and I want to learn more about the Indigenous people of Canada. Three years ago, I did the San'yas Indigenous Cultural Safety Program.

The homeless people of Whitechapel and the people of Cat Lake may live on different lands and dress differently than me but, their appreciation, kindness, compassion, and words of wisdom are rich beyond imagination. The resilience they cultivated in me is seen by those who said that I wouldn't like it here (Canada). I am grateful for having seen the faces of both communities and remember love instead of judgement. Thank you all for my awareness of the truth of, *"Don't Judge a Book By Its Cover."*

Nadira I. Dyalsingh

Nadira was born in Guyana and emigrated to England, where she started her Registered Nursing and Registered Midwifery careers. Later, she emigrated and settled in Ontario, Canada. Here she continues caring for the most vulnerable — newborn babies. Parents call her "The Baby Whisperer." From an impoverished community of East London, Nadira took her skills to the Northern Ontario Indigenous Community of Cat Lake, where gratitude and compassion flourish. Nadira can be seen discussing the topic of compassion on two of the *"707 Shows"*.

Here in Canada, Nadira has widened her interests to the psychology of colours and holistic care, assisting in bringing order, balance, and harmony to the energy fields of the weary. She uses the Colour Mirrors System, which was created by Melissie Jolly of South Africa and taught by Moira Bush in Canada, and Therapeutic Touch, founded by nurses Dolores Krieger and Dora Kunz. Therapeutic Touch is a healing modality that is practised in many health care facilities here in Toronto and around the world.

Thanks to Robert J. Moore, Nadira is a 2020 Guinness Book of World Records participant for the most authors signing the same book at the same time. Nadira loves teaching, sharing her knowledge, researching to find answers, spending quiet moments in church, or walking in nature, among her many other interests. On a global scale, Nadira enjoys communicating with family and friends.

Nadira can be contacted at:
Email: dyalsingh1803@rogers.com
LinkedIn: Nadira Dyalsingh
Instagram: @nadiradyalsingh
Facebook messenger: Nadira Dyalsingh

Award-Winning Publicist, Author, and Media Powerhouse

Bruce Serbin

I often think about what it would be like if I could go back in time and tell my younger self that I would become an entrepreneur. The Bruce of 20 years ago probably wouldn't believe it. I was a shy kid, the quiet one and a worrier. I wasn't one to stir the pot. These are probably not the characteristics most people think of when they hear the word entrepreneur. That's why it's not surprising that my journey to becoming an entrepreneur was by accident.

It was 2010 and the United States was starting to climb out of one of the worst recessionary periods ever. The public relations firm I was working for was in trouble. They were losing clients, money and laying off staff. My time with the company was fast approaching its end; I knew I needed to do something and quickly.

One day, I was speaking with one of our clients whom I had become friendly with and told him that I was being laid off and someone else would be working on his account. He said, "Bruce, you're really good at what you do. Why don't you go out and start your own company?" I laughed.

"Who me? Yeah, right," but he was serious, and he said he would bring his business to my company and refer others to me.

I looked at my options:

I could go back to where I started, working in TV news, but I didn't want to do that. I got burnt out on local news years ago; covering murders, robberies and car accidents wasn't appealing to me anymore.

I could find a job at another public relations firm. Then again, I had worked so hard to climb to the top of the firm that was about to lay me off, and I didn't want to start all over again as an account executive.

Perhaps, something unrelated? I like being a publicist and helping people get coverage in the media and building their credibility.

Or follow the advice of this client and start my own business? I guess so. I didn't know what else to do.

It was my very first day at it, and my only client, the one who followed me from the firm, calls me up and says,

"How was the traffic this morning?" Keep in mind; I was running the business out of my spare bedroom. Despite his laid-back and jovial attitude, I felt lost and full of doubt.

Could I do this on my own? Would I be able to continue to secure the same high-level media placements for this client? Could I grow the business? Forget about growing it; could I even survive? What do you mean Friday isn't payday anymore? You mean to say I have to be the bookkeeper and stay on top of the finances, play the role of the publicist and serve my clients, become a salesman and get new clients, create a website, be the janitor and everything else? It was overwhelming, to say the least.

I don't remember where I began, but I jumped right in. I started working even more aggressively with the one client I had, and it showed. The results were impressive, but more importantly, I proved to myself that I could do this on my own. Through ups and downs, good times and bad, here I am nine years later still doing my own thing. I wrote a book. I travel around the country and speak at events. I took advantage of every opportunity that came my way, big or small. I've worked with a lot of interesting people and learned so much about so many different topics. It's been one heck of a ride.

The Lessons I Learned

If you're reading Magnetic Entrepreneur, you're probably already an entrepreneur or at least considering becoming one. Either way, here are some of the lessons I learned along the way. I hope they can help you.

You will have days where you're on fire. You're at the top of your game, and nobody can stand in your way. Your clients are happy. Your business is booming. Everyone loves you.

You will have days where you want to run away and hide. You're going to have a trail of losses. You're going to lose clients. Your business will be in the toilet. You'll have no money. It will seem like no one wants anything to do with you.

Find the right emotional balance. When you're successful, celebrate and take pride in your achievements, but don't ever let it go to your head. On those days that you feel like the biggest failure in the world, remember that it's only temporary. Try to use it as a learning experience. In fact, most successful entrepreneurs will admit they've had more failures than successes. Remember, your next big success is right around the corner.

Keep your head on your shoulders. When you're running a business, everyone wants to sell you something. They will tell you that you need to do this or that to succeed. It's important to learn from others, but there's no "one size fits all" formula. Figure out what will work best for you.

Take a break. Most entrepreneurs love what they do. In fact, it doesn't even feel like work. It's easy to get so caught up and work for 14 hours straight. It's also unhealthy. Get away from it; Go on vacation; Spend time with family; Hang out with your friends; Do something fun; Get rid of your stress. The business will survive. Unless I'm working on a big breaking news story and I'm up against a tight deadline, I call it a day at the same time every day.

Don't compare yourself to other entrepreneurs. This was a tough one for me and something I still battle with from time to time. Early on, I got a few good breaks and met some very successful entrepreneurs. They taught me so much, but I started comparing myself to them and it set me back. I would think, "Why can they do this or that, but I can't? Why are they making 10 times more money than me? Why do

they have so many more clients than me?" There will always be someone who seems much farther along than you, and that's okay. Don't beat yourself up over it.

Third-party validation is king. It's one thing for me to tell someone they should hire me, but when someone else advises that person that they need to hire me, or even speaks highly of me; it's something entirely different. It holds much more clout. Not long ago, I spoke at an event put on by Larry Winget, better known as "The Pitbull of Personal Development." I made a short sales pitch at the end of my speech, and nobody cared. Larry came on stage and started singing my praises and I instantly had a line of people waiting to work with me. That's the biggest appeal about the media: instant third-party credibility.

Success is different for everyone. Many people tend to equate success with money and it is easy to focus on that as an entrepreneur, but it isn't everything. Granted, you need money to keep your business alive, but success is more than just money. I consider myself to be one of the most successful publicists in terms of securing media placements for my clients, but I'm not the wealthiest.

My favourite quote that is true in business and life:

"Be nicer than necessary to everyone you meet.

Everyone is fighting some kind of battle."

- Socrates

If I can make it, so can you. Just keep pushing your way in, and don't give up.

The Media: How and Why

Entrepreneurs are always looking for that competitive edge that makes them stand out and puts them at the top of their industry. One of the best ways to accomplish this is by consistently appearing in the media. When you're featured on radio, television, in newspapers, magazines and by online media outlets, it is the ultimate form of credibility. Having your insights highlighted by the press and aligning your name with local and national media outlets sends a message that you are truly an expert in your field. It is a silent endorsement from that media outlet that states you have something important to say, that you are smart, and again, that you are indeed an expert.

If you want to be a true magnetic entrepreneur, here's how to start attracting more media opportunities your way.

Serve as an expert source

The #1 reason people can't generate media coverage is that they make it a sales pitch or advertisement about themselves. Instead of making the focus of your media pitch about you, focus on an important topic and serve as an expert to explain it. The media is looking for tips, insights and actionable items that can help their viewers, readers or listeners understand a topic. Be that expert voice for the media.

Say something different, bold or controversial

If you are conveying the same message as 99% of your competition, why should the media focus on you? Say something different, take the other side of an issue and don't be afraid to be controversial. One crucial point to this is: be prepared to back up your point of view.

Focus on current events

One of the best ways to generate media coverage is to tie your message to current events. What topics are happening in your area of expertise that the media will be covering? The key is to act quickly with breaking news and offer yourself as a source to comment on the current events. Be a proactive source for the media because if they can't find you when they need you, they will find someone else.

Keep pitching new angles

Publicity is a process that takes time and is often filled with the rejection of your ideas from reporters, editors and producers. It's imperative to keep coming up with fresh angles with which to approach the media. Just because you don't get any bites on the first few tries, don't give up. Change your pitch, find a new angle or say something different and keep trying. It takes time and persistence.

Contribute articles

What most people don't realize about magazines and online news outlets is that they are always looking for informative and original articles to use from outside contributors. Write an informative piece on a topic in your area of expertise and then offer the article to magazine and online editors. Generally, you won't get paid for these submissions, but make sure to include a one-paragraph bio

with a link back to your webpage that will run at the end of the article.

Know how to write for the media

Television news, for example, is written on an elementary school level. Keep it simple, not too technical and watch your grammar. Open with a catchy and to-the- point sentence. Break up monotonous paragraphs with some bullet points. It's okay to "sexy" your message up a bit, but never lie and make promises you can't deliver on.

Know your audience

Most of my clients love the opportunity to be interviewed on television. It is still the most popular of any media and with good reason. The reality is while everyone can benefit from media exposure, TV may not be the best way to reach your target audience. Make sure you're aiming for the correct audience and also the media outlets that will be interested in interviewing you. There is a tremendous amount of credibility in radio, newspapers, magazines and online news sites and blogs. Every message is different and needs to be treated as such.

Leverage your media

After you start generating publicity, leverage it every way you possibly can. Sadly, most people don't take advantage of this. There are endless ways to do this: on your social media, by building an 'in the news' section on your website, sharing it with your database, in the intro to your speeches, via blog posts and more.

I want to wish you success on your journey as an entrepreneur. If I can do anything to help you along the way, feel free to reach out to me directly at bruce@serbinmedia.com You can learn more about me at www.serbinmedia.com.

If you're ready to start generating your own media coverage but don't have the time or budget to work with a professional publicist, check out my DIY media program at www.attractingmedia.com. As a special friend of Robert J. Moore and for reading this book, use coupon code 'Moore' at checkout for special pricing.

Bruce Serbin

For more than 15 years, eight-time national award-winning publicist and author, Bruce Serbin has been a media powerhouse, booking his clients on local and national television, radio shows, newspapers and magazines, and online news outlets. Bruce is the author of 30 Reasons The Media is Ignoring You: Deathbed Confessions of An Award-Winning Publicist www.serbinmediabook.com which has been described as the bible for generating media attention. He is also the founder of Attracting Media.com, an online DIY program that helps people secure publicity.

Bruce started his career in the newsroom working as a news assignment editor and producer writing anchor scripts for the evening news. He can write and pitch a compelling news story that gets past the newsroom gatekeeper because he was the gatekeeper. As a result, his clients are regularly featured in media outlets including: NBC's Today, ABC's Good Morning America, CNN, the Associated Press, the BBC, Reuters, The New York Times, Forbes, TIME and more.

In 2008, he founded Serbin Media, Inc. www.serbinmedia.com, a publicity firm that serves clients in fields from financial services and the travel industry to authors, business consultants, speakers and many others. Bruce has been involved in media campaigns with celebrities that include Nick Cannon from *"America's Got Talent,"* Kevin Harrington from *"Shark Tank,"* Dr. Buck Parker from *"The Island"* and the band *"One Direction."*

In addition to his role as a media publicist, Bruce is also a trainer and consultant working with companies to improve their media and PR programs. He has delivered programs to large corporations as well as entrepreneurial audiences and keynoted for the National Speaker's Association Million-Dollar Roundtable. He has shared the stage with some of the world's top speakers, including Bob Proctor, Brian Tracy, and Steve Siebold. He was featured in Forbes, Entrepreneur, Business News Daily and Yahoo.

Conclusion

Thank you for reading this book. Every co-author has worked hard to bring not only their stories but also valuable lessons that you can use to become magnetic yourself.

One of the best ways to become magnetic is to become an author yourself, and I would love to help you with that. If you would like to be a part of *The Magnetic Entrepreneur* book series, please contact my team at:

Email - info@magneticentrepreneurinc.com
Linkedin - www.linkedin.com/in/magneticentrepreneur
Facebook - Magnetic Entrepreneur Inc.

Become more than you can ever imagine!

Robert J. Moore

-5X Internationally Awarded / Bestselling Author of:
From Rock Bottom to Success and
The Better Way Formula – Principles for Success and *Magnetic Entrepreneur* book series, Publisher
CEO and Founder of Magnetic Entrepreneur Inc., ™
Guinness World Record holder
Nominee Walk of Fame, Canada   International Speaker

CPSIA information can be obtained
at www.ICGtesting.com
Printed in the USA
LVHW081809231021
701314LV00014B/821